Sustainable Careers

Navigating Career Options for a Resilient and Sustainable Future

Liz Painter

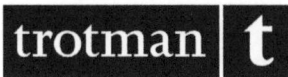

Sustainable Careers

This first edition published in 2025 by Trotman, an imprint of Trotman Indigo Publishing Ltd, 18e Charles Street, Bath BA1 1HX

© Trotman Indigo Publishing Ltd 2025

Author: Liz Painter

British Library Cataloguing in Publication Data
A catalogue record for this book is available from the British Library

Paperback ISBN 978 1 911724 53 7
eISBN 978 1 911724 54 4

All rights reserved. This book is sold subject to the condition that it shall not, by way of trade or otherwise, be lent, resold, hired out or otherwise circulated without the publisher's prior written consent in any form of binding or cover other than that in which it is published and without a similar condition including this condition being imposed on the subsequent purchaser. No part of this publication may be reproduced, stored in a retrieval system or transmitted in any form or by any means, electronic and mechanical, photocopying, recording or otherwise without prior permission of Trotman Indigo Publishing.

Every effort has been made to trace copyright holders and to obtain their permission for the use of copyright material. The publisher apologises for any errors or omissions, and would be grateful to be notified of any corrections that should be incorporated in future editions of this book.

The authorised representative in the EEA is Easy Access System Europe Oü (EAS), Mustamäe tee 50, 10621 Tallinn, Estonia.

Printed and bound in the UK by CMP Ltd.

 All details in this book were correct at the time of going to press. To keep up to date with all the latest news and updates and to access the online resources that accompany this book, use this QR code or visit **www.trotman.co.uk/pages/sustainable-careers-resources**

Contents

About the author	vii
Acknowledgements	ix
Foreword	xiii
Introducing the book and the *Golden Thread*	1
Chapter 1 Setting the scene	**3**
Introduction	3
What is sustainability?	3
Futureproofing for a sustainable career	4
Why is the 'green transition' important?	5
What is net zero?	6
This isn't just about science, technology, engineering and maths (STEM)	7
A jingle-jangle of terms	7
Why is sustainability important?	8
Further ways this book will help you	8
Conclusion	9
Chapter 2 The United Nations Sustainable Development Goals	**11**
Introduction	11
Why are the SDGs important in career development work?	12
Table 2.1. Overview of the 17 SDGs and how each can support career education	13
Taking this further	15
Table 2.2. Mapping the Gatsby Foundation's eight benchmarks of Good Career Guidance (England) to the SDGs	16
Mapping the SDGs to other career development frameworks	16
Table 2.3. Mapping the CDI Career Development Framework to the SDGs	16
Progress towards Agenda 2030	17
Using the SDGs to transform career development work	17
Conclusion	18
Chapter 3 A sustainable career	**21**
Introduction	21
Definitions of career	22
Career development	24
Learning is lifelong	27
Decent work	28

Work and well-being	29
Green guidance	31
Skills	32
Green skills – a big idea	33
Green jobs	35
Sustainability and the workforce	36
Conclusion	36

Chapter 4   Careers in sustainability (types of green jobs)   39

Introduction	39
1. New green and energy occupations	41
2. Green enhanced	42
3. Green increased demand occupations	44
4. And everyone else's job	45
Conclusion	47

Chapter 5   Sectors getting us to net zero   49

Introduction	49
Energy	50
What is happening with fossil fuels?	52
Renewable energy	53
Nuclear energy	54
Hydrogen	55
The 'National Grid'	57
Electricity providers	57
Jobs in the energy sector	58
Water and waste management	59
The water industry	59
Jobs in the water industry	60
Waste management	61
The circular economy	62
Jobs in the waste management industry	63
Conservation	65
Biodiversity	65
Natural carbon capture	66
Water	66
Mini case study – Woodland Trust, Glen Finglas Estate	67
Careers in conservation	67
Conclusion	69

Chapter 6   Sectors working in a sustainable way   71

| Introduction | 71 |
| Sectors | 72 |

Mineral products	73
Agriculture and food	74
Construction	75
Manufacturing	78
Health	80
Creative industries sector	81
Conclusion	83
Case Study 1 – Balfour Beatty	84

Chapter 7 Qualifications in sustainability — **91**

Introduction	91
Training for teachers and career professionals	92
Secondary school courses	93
Sustainability qualifications in England and Northern Ireland	94
Mini case study: Eastern Education Group, Suffolk	96
Further education	98
Undergraduate courses	98
Postgraduate study	99
Sector specific	100
Conclusion	101
Case Study 2 – Luke, University Estates Sustainability Officer	102

Chapter 8 Rising to the challenge — **107**

Introduction	107
Political thinking	108
We're off track	108
Money, money, money	109
What about jobs?	112
Education	113
Are you ready?	113
Supporting young people	114
Disruptors	115
Conclusion	116
Case Study 3 – PEEQUAL, an entrepreneurial company	117

Chapter 9 Sustainability and career education — **123**

Introduction	123
Frame it!	124
1. The 17 Sustainable Development Goals (SDGs)	124
2. The CDI Career Development Framework	125
3. Environmentally sustainable career guidance	125
Table 9.1. Dimsits and Hooley's' five dimensions for environmentally sustainable career guidance	126

Make it relevant	128
Student-centred	131
Types of activity	133
Table 9.2. Overview of a suggested progressive and sustainable SDE programme	133
Figure 9.1. Planning for a sustainable careers education programme	135
Table 9.3. Things to consider when planning activities	135
Table 9.4. Suggested sustainable development education activities for curriculum areas	136
Subject-specific activities	137
Mini case study: WWF-UK Sustainable Futures programme	137
Mini Case Study: Climate Action Plans and Suffolk education	139
Sustainability Governor	141
School Business Leadership	142
Conclusion	142
Case Study 4 – Bedford Academy	143
Selection of resources for schools and colleges	148

Chapter 10   Wrapping up — 151

Introduction	151
Why is the topic of sustainability important?	152
Why do young people need to learn about having a sustainable career?	152
Table 10.1. The nine planetary boundaries	153
There are challenges	154
Planning your next steps	154
Table 10.2. Example of a SWOT analysis for an individual teacher or career professional	155
Table 10.3. Example of a SWOT analysis for an educational programme	156
Conclusion	156

References for each chapter — 157

About the author

Liz Painter is a freelance career development professional, has an MA in Careers Education and Coaching and is registered with the CDI.

She was a science teacher for 24 years and led a range of STEM activities across the school, including clubs, cross-curricular collaboration days and STEM in PSHCE programmes. Liz was invited to speak at two Inside Government conferences about encouraging girls into STEM careers.

After leaving teaching in 2019, she joined the Cheshire and Warrington LEP where she supported schools with their careers education programme and facilitated employer engagement activities. In 2021, Liz began to concentrate on her freelance portfolio. She delivers training and creates resources for teachers, helping to bring career learning into the classroom. Liz has worked on projects for a number of organisations, including STEM Learning, developing career-related resources for educators and young people.

Liz's personal interests involve supporting environmental charities and trying to live more sustainably. Researching for the second edition of STEM Careers led Liz to develop a deeper understanding of sustainability and its intersection between our career, industry and the planet.

A successful career in science teaching and the academic knowledge of career development puts Liz in the unique position of understanding what both teachers and young people will find useful in supporting the transition from education into employment.

Acknowledgements

I had the idea for this book as I was writing *STEM Careers* (2nd edition). Thank you to Trotman for listening to my ideas and inviting me to write a book proposal. I knew this book had to be more than 'jobs to build wind turbines'; having the mindset to keep one's career sustainable and improving sustainable development education are also important interpretations of 'sustainability and careers'.

In July 2024 the National Institute for Career Education and Counselling held a conference focusing on 'career and sustainability', and it was so exciting to hear people talking about the importance of green guidance, lifelong working and decent work. If you haven't seen the journal based on the event, I can heartily recommend reading it.

https://nicecjournal.co.uk/index.php/nc/issue/view/53/56

Thank you to the many people who have read sections of the book and offered guidance, especially William E. Donald, Karen Cannard, Nigel Royal, Connie Young, Nicola Simons, Tristram Hooley and Miriam Dimsits. A book of this relatively short length covering such big topics is bound to have a few subjective perspectives and simplifications, and facts could be out of date at the time of publishing. All errors are therefore my own.

Dedication

This book is dedicated to my husband, Andy, and daughter, Caitlin. Thank you for supporting me once again as I write a book, supplying cups of tea, reading drafts and providing your insights from the world of work.

Foreword

The theme of sustainability in careers is one that has been growing in career education and guidance in recent years and is one that is likely only to grow in prominence. Liz Painter's book is timely therefore, offering a comprehensive overview of the subject that will be of great interest to careers leaders, career development professionals, educators and policymakers alike.

Readers looking for support with developing the sustainability element within their school's or college's careers education programmes will find this volume to be a rich source of information. As Painter makes clear, sustainability is not a theme relevant only to STEM subjects; all subjects (and all sectors) have their role to play in helping mitigate environmental harm and can help individuals develop the skills and values needed to help employers – and society as a whole – make the shift towards a more sustainable future.

Career development professionals will find a wealth of up-to-date occupational information on the key sectors leading the way in the transition to net zero. This includes sectors that most readers would expect to be involved in these efforts (e.g. the energy industry, water and waste management, and conservation) as well as industries as diverse as retail, hospitality and tourism and the creative industries. Practitioners will find this to be very valuable when supporting clients interested in the environmental impact of their career choices.

As one would expect from a book focused on sustainability, Painter ensures that the readers are fully apprised of 'the big picture' throughout. As well as drawing on the most up-to-date research on the subject, this book situates the topic in the light of important global initiatives such as the United Nations Sustainable Development Goals. Nevertheless, Painter always maintains a practice-orientated focus, providing useful suggestions for how the readers can embed this wider perspective on sustainability in careers education programmes and in interactions with clients.

This book represents an important contribution to the literature on career development practice and also to the field of education for sustainable development. I have no hesitation in recommending it to readers interested in either subject, or in both.

Dr Oliver Jenkin PGCE RCDP, NICEC Fellow
Career Development Professional and Editor of the CDI's magazine, Career Matters,
May 2025

Introducing the book and the *Golden Thread*

A book about sustainability and careers covers complex ideas and can be a confusing landscape. There are three main themes throughout this book:

1. **Sustainability and careers:** The types of 'green jobs' and skills required for sectors to reduce their greenhouse gas emissions and encourage nature restoration. Chapters 4, 5, 6 and 7 are the main parts of the book with this focus.
2. **A sustainable career:** Preparing young people for a sustainable career that gives them decent work and prepares them for lifelong learning that doesn't negatively affect their mental health. This is discussed in detail in chapters 3, 8 and 9.
3. **Sustainable development education (SDE):** Teaching *about* and teaching *for* sustainable development. Chapters 2, 7 and 9 provide the focus for this.

These are all held together with the 'golden thread' of the United Nations Sustainability Goals.

It is hoped that this book will be a practical guide, inspiring you to develop your understanding of sustainability and enhance your teaching and career guidance practice. Within the text you'll find three types of activities for use in the classroom and with individual clients to help you take the next steps:

- **World of work examples** with suggestions of how these can be useful for a teacher or career professional.
- **Things to think about** including questions for reflection.
- **Interesting facts** that could be useful when talking with young people about sustainability and the world of work.

There are four main case studies included that provide real-life examples of sustainability in the workplace. These stories are to help you widen your knowledge of business and sustainability in the workplace so that you can share this information with young people. I am grateful to the people who gave their time to be interviewed for the book.

- **Case Study 1:** Balfour Beatty's approach to sustainability (end of chapter 6).
- **Case Study 2:** Career story of Luke, a sustainability manager (end of chapter 7).
- **Case Study 3:** PEEQUAL, an entrepreneurial company solving a problem (end of chapter 8).
- **Case Study 4:** Bedford Academy, a school with sustainable development at its heart (end of chapter 9).

Chapter 1
Setting the scene

> The world of work is changing, and young people are more aware than ever of local and global issues and they want to feel empowered to contribute.

Introduction

How can we help prepare our young people for their future careers when the world is changing so fast that we can struggle to keep up ourselves? With new technologies, employers' responses to the climate debate and an individual's well-being high on the agenda, those who support young people have many new ideas to digest to be helpful.

This book is for teachers, career professionals, parents, carers and anyone who works with young people. It will help you to understand the complex arena of 'sustainable careers' so that you can help young people navigate this. The book could also be useful for adults who want to explore their career development and understand more about careers in sustainability.

The aim of this book is to give you the information, or signposts to further knowledge, to help you feel more confident when you inform and guide young people about sustainability and careers. We can help them to have the mindset and career management skills to flourish in the changing world of work.

The book will also be beneficial for those who develop career education strategies. There will be practical guidance to help you create an inspiring careers programme relevant to the environmental and social issues of today, which is itself sustainable, year on year.

What is sustainability?

The answer is not as straightforward as you may think.

The *Cambridge Dictionary* has two definitions of sustainability:

- 'the quality of being able to continue over a period of time' and
- 'the quality of causing little or no damage to the environment and therefore able to continue for a long time'.

The *Oxford Dictionary* also has two definitions:

- 'the use of natural products and energy in a way that does not harm the environment' and
- 'the ability to continue or be continued for a long time'.

They seem quite similar and yet different. Both concur that 'continuing over a long period of time' is key, yet 'environment' is included in one and 'natural products and energy' are mentioned in the other. Neither source references economics but we know that natural products, energy and, more recently, the environment have a monetary value.

A quick search of the internet will show that most organisations refer to the three pillars of sustainability as economic, environmental and social. Purvis, Mao and Robinson (2019) reviewed many academic papers and reports to try and pin down when the concept of the 'three pillars of sustainability' first appeared, and they struggled.[1] They also found no common consensus about how the three factors interplay, for example, are they hierarchical or interconnected? This is a complex topic, so no wonder some of us feel a little out of our depth when we think about supporting clients and young people.

So, using the dictionary definitions and the three pillars of sustainability, for this book, **sustainability is about economic, environmental and social factors having a minimum negative impact on future generations.** Often the portrayal of this in the media is foreboding, concentrating on the negative consequences of human impact on the planet. Let's promote the positives of sustainability – the success stories and the opportunities. If we can help young people understand that each factor is important, it can help them to make informed decisions that link with their values and interests (in life, in general, and their careers).

Futureproofing for a sustainable career

We can also consider sustainability from the perspective of the individual and their career. The main focus of chapter 3 will be ways to help young people develop their career management skills so that they will be able to thrive during their, hopefully, long working lives.

We are living in disruptive times. The ongoing development of artificial intelligence (AI) and digitisation in the workplace alongside the effects of geopolitics and globalisation all have the potential to affect all of our careers. The individual is at the centre of this. Helping young people to have the skills to 'futureproof' their careers is more than discussing employability. Developing their psychological capital (such as personal resilience and self-efficacy), social capital (so they can move out of their comfort zone with some confidence) and human capital (competencies, knowledge and skills) is intrinsic.

Why is the 'green transition' important?

It is undeniable that human activity has affected the climate, environment and biodiversity on the planet. Many governments and organisations declare this a crisis. This can feel scary for young people as they may feel powerless to be able to effect change. Every individual and organisation has a part to play in improving things, and, as adults who support young people, we are well placed to help them see the importance of redressing the crisis issues and the opportunities this may afford.

In 2019, the WWF, in partnership with the UK's Institute for Public Policy Research, produced a series of inspiring essays in a collection called 'Putting people at the heart of the green transition'.[2] The green transition is the move towards addressing the problems caused by human activity, including climate change, loss of biodiversity and the environmental impact on water, air and land. Academics, politicians, entrepreneurs, conservationists and business people discuss the role of the economy, policy, society and, especially, young people in the green transition and the call to action for a fair and just transition for all.

Things to think about

The 'Putting people at the heart of the green transition' collection of essays could form an interesting conversation starter for young people today.[2]

How far have these ideas come since 2019?

What role can they play in the green transition, and what do they need to be able to do to make a difference?

The European Training Foundation (ETF) produced a report in 2022 called 'Skills for the green transition'.[3] The ETF states that it's important that the transition is fair, 'leaving no one behind'. In reviewing green transition policies from across the continent, the ETF finds that while many governments have ambitious plans, the role of education and skill development in driving this transition is overlooked. Chapter 3 will discuss the range of skills desired by employers, with an emphasis on 'green skills'.

Success requires strategic leadership, cooperation, collaboration and innovation and involves all parts of society:

- Academics – use research to provide evidence.
- Governments – use the evidence to develop legislation and policies for their countries.
- Profit-making organisations – use the legislation and policies to develop strategies to comply with while maintaining a profit.
- Non-profit organisations – use the legislation and policies to develop strategies and activities that directly contribute to the green transition.
- Individuals – each doing their bit to support their 'organisation' (e.g. work, local council or home).

What is net zero?

Over the last 200 years, human activities have rapidly increased the amount of carbon dioxide (CO_2) being released into the atmosphere. This gas, along with others such as methane and nitrous oxide, is known as a 'greenhouse gas'. The natural greenhouse effect is what keeps our planet at the correct temperature to sustain life. However, the excess gases that humans are producing (called anthropogenic) are causing global temperatures to rise and the climate to rapidly change.[4] Students in the UK learn about this in the science and geography curricula, but if you feel you need a bit of a refresher, the British Geological Survey has some interesting information that is evidence based.[5]

The UK government acknowledges that climate change is occurring due to human activities, and although temperature increase may only be small (average of 1.1°C since pre-industrial times), the effects are great. Habitats on land and in the oceans are being affected causing a decrease in biodiversity. Changing climate conditions may affect water and food security, and human health may be affected due to heat stress.[5]

The overwhelming evidence of the effects of anthropogenic climate change has led to governments producing policies to reduce greenhouse gas emissions. In 2021, the UK government published its Net Zero Strategy.[6] The term net zero means balancing greenhouse gas emissions with their removal from the atmosphere, and as explained in the UK's Net Zero Strategy document, the government aims to achieve this by 2050. Removal, sometimes referred to as carbon capture, involves either plants using CO_2 or humans developing technology to remove the CO_2. Increasing the use of removal techniques does not mean we can keep on emitting high levels of greenhouse gases. Industry and individuals, encouraged by the UK government's strategies, will all need to be involved, and this requires behavioural change and innovation. The energy transition is a huge part of our transition to net zero, and this will be discussed further in chapter 5.

Solving climate change is a complex issue. Changing how people and organisations work and behave can lead to conflict. Some sectors such as aviation may be more difficult to decarbonise, and the methods used to calculate whether a country, organisation or home has achieved net zero may not be transparent. Social commentators are concerned that the energy transition will negatively affect the poorer members of our society if improved technologies and upgrades are priced outside of their income. Chapter 8 will examine the challenges, conflicts and solutions and how these can affect our careers and career decision-making.

(See the resources section at the end of this chapter for links to the net zero strategies for Scotland, Northern Ireland and Wales.)

This isn't just about science, technology, engineering and maths (STEM)

Climate mitigation is everyone's responsibility, and careers linked to sustainability are available for all. This isn't just for STEM students. Employers will increasingly look for employees who share their values towards achieving a net zero business. For many companies, their main focus will be on innovating and developing solutions to help the country, and the world, reverse the negative effects of human activities. Human-centric skills such as problem-solving, creativity and critical thinking are highly valued: chapter 3 will consider this in greater depth.

All industry sectors and job roles have a part to play in reducing carbon emissions, helping the UK to achieve net zero by 2050. This book will help you support young people interested in media, finance, the law, the arts, music, charity work, sport and every subject, to find meaningful careers and develop the mindset to consider how their work impacts the planet for future generations.

A jingle-jangle of terms

Green, environmental and sustainability? This book will use the core term *sustainable*, as it includes economic, environmental and social factors that affect individuals, organisations and society. Help your young people see past the buzzwords and understand what the implications are. This is a complex topic with many terms (e.g. green skills and jobs). Categorising them is difficult, and the layout in this book proposes one way of doing this. This book can't include every 'green' job, or how every job can become 'green', but will help to identify key skills required by employers, the emerging job roles and sectors leading the sustainability cause.

Why is sustainability important?

Put simply, to help make a fairer world for all – individuals, society and nature. Whether you are thinking locally and want the best for your students, or aspire that your young adults will transition into further education and the world of work with a global mindset and strong sense of social justice, thinking, living and working sustainably is important. Collective action, including career development work, can help the planet to recover, and the response in the late 20th century to the depletion of the ozone layer is a successful example of global cooperation.

The United Nations Sustainable Development Goals (UN SDGs) were created as a framework for governments worldwide, but we can also use this as a resource with the career development work we do with students and clients. Chapter 2 will focus on how teachers and career development practitioners can use the UN SDGs.

Climate anxiety, also referred to as ecoanxiety, is a real phenomenon that is experienced by a growing number of young people. We need to reduce this by empowering young people and giving them the agency to make a difference.[7] But we can't burden the individual. This is a task for all of society, and we all have a role to play in helping young people to be part of solving the problems. This will be discussed further in chapter 8.

The labour market is an important topic in the discussion about climate change. In chapter 4 we'll explore that there are relatively few new types of green jobs; some jobs will disappear but most will require new skills.

Further ways this book will help you

Sustainability is a hot topic. So, it is important to help young people become critical thinkers, understand concepts such as 'greenwashing' and 'green hushing' and be able to evaluate information from different sectors, industries and companies against their values and interests. Strategies to help you with this will be discussed in chapters 2, 3 and 9.

Chapters 4, 5 and 6 will focus on jobs, sectors, industries and organisations that are supporting sustainability, nature recovery and the transition to net zero. The case study about Balfour Beatty shows how a major company is addressing sustainability.

Chapter 7 will focus on practical ways for educators and career professionals to learn about sustainable development education and the variety of qualifications that can lead to a career in sustainability. The case study about Luke offers stories that can be used to inform and inspire young people.

Titled 'Rising to the challenge', chapter 8 focuses on the potential challenges, tensions and conflicts as society strives for reduced carbon emissions, nature restoration and a 'just' transition:

- for teachers and career professionals incorporating sustainability into their practice;
- for young people as they navigate their early careers; and
- for businesses trying to remain economically viable.

Chapter 9 will support practitioners, in education and careers, helping you develop (excuse the pun) a 'Sustainable Careers Strategy' that supports your young people, year after year – with information about activities and external agency resources that you can incorporate into the delivery of your careers education programme.

Chapter 10 brings everything together and will help you to plan your next steps, as this changing world offers exciting opportunities for our young people, whatever their ability, background or interests.

Conclusion

Careers in sustainability and sustainable careers are more than buzzwords; they are important concepts for us to understand so that we can help young people navigate this complex landscape.

To start, ensure you have a good grasp of how human activities since industrialisation are affecting the world's climate, habitats and therefore biodiversity, food and water security. Understanding how this affects people and society and how the economy drives, or inhibits, change is also beneficial.

Scientific evidence is used by world organisations and governments to change legislation so that we can reduce our negative impact on the planet. Help students to see that innovating new technologies and changing the way organisations work provide exciting career opportunities in all sectors.

The changes will affect us all, and we want our young people to be at the forefront of a 'just' transition that is inclusive and leaves no one behind.

From learning how to manage our careers in a changing world so that we have rewarding and meaningful work to understanding how the changes in technology will affect our day-to-day lives, this book will give you the tools to support young people.

Change can be daunting, but it can also provide opportunities and for those of us who work with young people, it is important to promote the positives. All of the technological developments and environmental restorations have the potential to improve society and make the world a better place for us now and in the future – the definition of sustainability.

Many organisations use the UN SDGs to guide their sustainability practice. The next chapter will focus on the SDGs, as they are a 'blueprint to achieve a better and more sustainable future for all'.[8] We will explore how the goals can be used as a framework to guide career development work, helping young people to consider how their careers can have a positive impact, whether locally or internationally.

Definitions used in this book

Sustainable development

Meeting the needs of the present without compromising the ability of future generations to meet their own needs.

(Adapted from www.iisd.org/mission-and-goals/sustainable-development)

Sustainable development education

Raising awareness about how today's actions affect the future, encouraging individuals to take responsible actions, to understand and address global and local challenges, such as climate change, loss of biodiversity and overuse of resources.

(Adapted from https://education.gov.scot/resources/learning-for-sustainability-advice-and-guidance/sustainable-development-education/)

A sustainable career

The jobs and roles a person has throughout their life, in work, home and society, driven by their personal choices and providing meaning to the individual.

(Adapted from De Vos, A. (2024). Enhancing the sustainability of careers in disruptive times. *Journal of the National Institute for Career Education and Counselling*, 53(1), 8–17. https://doi.org/10.20856/jnicec.5302)

Chapter 2
The United Nations Sustainable Development Goals

> A resource for career development and career education programmes.

Introduction

In chapter 1, the definitions and concepts of sustainability were introduced. The United Nations Sustainable Development Goals (SDGs) were developed from the Millennium Goals in 2015 and cover the three pillars of sustainable development: economic, social and environmental.

The 17 goals are interconnected and are the driving force behind Agenda 2030, an ambitious global plan for action that aims to eradicate poverty, support the human rights of everyone and protect the planet from further degradation by 2030.[1]

The main pledge of the SDGs is to 'leave no one behind'. This is both within and among countries, and the goals provide a framework for the governments of the 193 UN member states to devise economic, social and environmental policies that will enable this.[1]

The UK government and the home nations are committed to the delivery of the SDGs. Across all UK government departments, policies are in place that will, implicitly or explicitly, help the UK work towards achieving the goals.[2]

The ability of the devolved governments to legislate provides alternative approaches to improving society and the environment. In Wales, the SDGs are explicit in Future Wales, the National Plan 2040 framework 'setting the direction for development in Wales to 2040'. This framework embeds the Well-being of Future Generations (Wales) Act 2015.[3]

Things to think about

The UN encourages education and charity organisations to use the downloadable icons for each of the 17 goals.[4]

How could you make use of the downloadable icons?

Visit the website for more information https://sdgs.un.org/goals#icons.

Why are the SDGs important in career development work?

The SDGs are relevant to everyone.

The 17 goals are just as important to a young person in the UK as they are to people in all countries across the world. The goals can also help us to develop UK citizens with a global mindset, aware of the economic, social and cultural differences around the world. A global mindset in their employees is valued by many employers.

Teaching young people about Agenda 2030 and the 17 SDGs can empower them to be the enablers of the future, helping to improve society and the environment for the benefit of all. Teachers and career professionals can help young people explore how their subject interests, values and social concerns link to the goals and can lead to career exploration.

The SDGs can also be used on a more practical, individual level, helping young people to understand what decent work is and how it can help with well-being. Decent work, as defined by the International Labour Organization (ILO)[5], 'involves opportunities for work that is productive and delivers a fair income, security in the workplace and social protection for all, better prospects for personal development and social integration, freedom for people to express their concerns, organize and participate in the decisions that affect their lives and equality of opportunity and treatment for all women and men'. There is a short video you can share with students on the ILO website.[5]

In his briefing paper for the Career Development Institute (CDI), Pete Robinson explores how career development services can deliver public policies linked to the SDGs, mapping some of the goals onto six public policy objectives that career development work directly contributes to.[6] The author acknowledges that not all 17 goals directly relate to career development work, but Table 2.1 gives an overview of each SDG and how each could contribute to a careers education programme that supports a well-rounded school or college curriculum.

Chapter 2: The United Nations Sustainable Development Goals

Table 2.1. Overview of the 17 SDGs and how each can support career education

UN SDG[1]	Brief explanation[1]	Linking to career development	Possible link to sectors, careers and jobs
Goal 1 End poverty	End poverty in all its forms everywhere.	Social equity. Access to decent work.	Third sector. Local government.
Goal 2 Zero hunger	End hunger, achieve food security and improved nutrition and promote sustainable agriculture.	Social equity. Access to decent work.	Agri-food sector. Health and nutrition. Local government.
Goal 3 Good health and well-being	Ensure healthy lives and promote well-being for all at all ages.	Developing career management skills, such as decision-making. Good mental health awareness.	Healthcare. Science and technology. Third sector.
Goal 4 Quality education	Ensure inclusive and equitable quality education and promote lifelong learning opportunities for all.	Sustainable and progressive careers education programme that • challenges academic stereotypes; • encourages lifelong learning.	Education. Careers development profession.
Goal 5 Gender equality	Achieve gender equality and empower all women and girls.	Developing career management skills. Challenging stereotypes and providing access to positive role models.	Women in successful careers in *all* sectors. Third sector. Equality, diversity and inclusion roles.
Goal 6 Clean water and sanitation	Ensure availability and sustainable management of water and sanitation for all.	Exploring 'green guidance'. Exploring values.	Conservation. Science and technology. Urban development and infrastructure. Third sector.
Goal 7 Affordable and clean energy	Ensure access to affordable, reliable, sustainable and modern energy for all.	Exploring 'green guidance'. Exploring values.	Renewable and sustainable energy. Science and technology. Third sector.
Goal 8 Decent work and economic growth	Promote sustained, inclusive and sustainable economic growth, full and productive employment and decent work for all.	Understanding what decent work is. Exploring employment law. Labour market information (LMI).	Business management. Law. Careers development profession.
Goal 9 Industry, innovation and infrastructure	Build resilient infrastructure, promote inclusive and sustainable industrialisation and foster innovation.	Exploring 'green guidance'. Exploring values.	Mining and mineral products. Construction. Manufacturing. Logistics. Conservation. Science and technology.

(Continued)

Table 2.1 (Continued)

UN SDG[1]	Brief explanation[1]	Linking to career development	Possible link to sectors, careers and jobs
Goal 10 Reduced inequalities	Reduce inequality within and among countries.	Social equity. Challenging stereotypes and providing access to positive role models.	Third sector. Local government. International agencies (such as the United Nations). Equality, diversity and inclusion roles.
Goal 11 Sustainable cities and communities	Make cities and human settlements inclusive, safe, resilient and sustainable.	Exploring 'green guidance'. Exploring values.	Conservation. Construction. Urban planning. Police. Armed forces.
Goal 12 Responsible consumption and production	Ensure sustainable consumption and production patterns.	Exploring 'green guidance'. Link to subject learning in science, geography and technology.	Mining and mineral products. Manufacturing. Logistics.
Goal 13 Climate action	Take urgent action to combat climate change and its impacts.	Exploring 'green guidance'. Link to subject learning in science, geography and technology.	Conservation. Renewable energy. Academia (research).
Goal 14 Life below water	Conserve and sustainably use the oceans, seas and marine resources for sustainable development.	Exploring 'green guidance'. Link to subject learning in science and geography.	Agriculture and food. Maritime logistics. Conservation. Marine biology
Goal 15 Life on land	Protect, restore and promote sustainable use of terrestrial ecosystems, sustainably manage forests, combat desertification, halt and reverse land degradation and halt biodiversity loss.	Exploring 'green guidance'. Link to subject learning in science and geography.	Mining and mineral products. Agriculture and food. Construction. Logistics. Conservation.
Goal 16 Peace, justice and strong institutions	Promote peaceful and inclusive societies for sustainable development, provide access to justice for all and build effective, accountable and inclusive institutions at all levels.	Developing career management skills, such as decision-making. Exploring values.	Third sector. Education. Law. Police. Armed Forces.
Goal 17 Partnerships for the goals	Strengthen the means of implementation and revitalise the Global Partnership for Sustainable Development.	Exploring values and behaviours. Cross-curriculum work to model partnership working.	Education. Media. Local government. International agencies (such as the United Nations).

Suggestions are made of how each goal can link to career development, including subject-specific, and how each goal can link to exploring sectors, careers and jobs.

Taking this further

Are there other ways for careers leaders, practitioners and teachers to use the goals? If you work in a school or college you will probably have a career education strategy and programme. This may be embedded within a broader personal and social education programme. You can use the SDG to chart how broad, holistic and globally aware your programme is. The aim is not to find an activity for each goal but to critically consider if your programme addresses each of the 17 points that the UN identifies as contributing towards sustainable development.

To review existing strategies:

- Map each part of your career education strategy against the 17 SDGs.
- Identify any goals that you cannot reference in your existing strategy.
- Consider how any of these 'missing' goals could add more breadth or depth to your strategy.

To review existing education programmes:

- Map the activities in each part of your programme against the 17 SDGs.
- Identify any goals that you cannot reference on your existing programme.
- Identify points in your programme that these 'missing' goals could support, and add topics and activities that would contribute to the goals currently not covered.

Any programme of study should be regularly evaluated. What is working well? What needs to be improved? What needs to be added? How do we know? Chapters 9 and 10 will discuss evaluating careers education programmes in greater detail, but this next activity demonstrates how you can evaluate the impact of your programme contributing to your school's/college's SDGs objectives:

- Identify your school's/college's priorities.
- Identify the parts of your career education strategy that support these priorities.
- From the exercises above, find the SDGs mapped to your strategy that supports your school's priorities.
- Gather quantitative data and testimonial stories as evidence of impact.

Remember, a well-developed strategy will drive an impactful and sustainable programme. This should be progressive and allow students at all levels to develop their understanding of their place in a just and sustainable world.

Table 2.2. Mapping the Gatsby Foundation's eight benchmarks of Good Career Guidance (England) to the SDGs[7]

Gatsby benchmarks	UN SDG
1. A stable careers programme	All 17 goals
2. Learning from career and labour market information	Goals 6, 7, 8, 9, 11, 12
3. Addressing the needs of each pupil	Goals 1, 2, 3, 5, 10, 16
4. Linking curriculum learning to careers	Goals 3, 6, 7, 9, 11, 12, 13, 14, 15
5. Encounters with employers and employees	Goals 3, 6, 7, 9, 11, 12, 13, 14, 15
6. Experiences of the workplace	Goals 3, 6, 7, 9, 11, 12, 13, 14, 15
7. Encounters with further and higher education	Goals 4, 5, 10
8. Personal guidance	All 17 goals

The Gatsby benchmarks are statutory in England and used as a framework for good career guidance in schools and colleges.

Read the case study in chapter 9 to see how Bedford Academy uses the SDGs in the operation of the school and the education of its students.

Mapping the SDGs to other career development frameworks

This is a subjective exercise and your opinions may differ from the mapping ideas presented. However, doing the mapping exercise is a good way to think about, and interrogate, different elements within a framework or programme. It can also help you to identify any areas that may be overlooked in your existing career education strategy and programmes.

If you are a career professional or teaching in Scotland, could you map the Curriculum for Excellence against the SDGs? For colleagues in Wales, Careers and the World of Work framework could be mapped against the SDGs. Those working in schools in Northern Ireland may want to map the goals against the Preparing for Success careers strategy.

Table 2.3. Mapping the CDI Career Development Framework[8] to the SDGs

The CDI six learning areas	UN SDGs
Grow throughout life	Goals 4, 5, 10, 16
Explore possibilities	Goals 4, 8
Manage career	Goals 4, 8
Create opportunities	Goals 3, 4, 16, 17
Balance life and work	Goals 3, 4, 5, 8, 10, 11
See the big picture	All 17 goals

The CDI's Career Development Framework has been designed for use across the UK for primary, secondary and post-16 students.

From this exercise, the 17 SDGs are not overtly linked to all six learning areas in the CDI Framework, and Goals 1, 2, 6, 7, 9, 12, 13, 14 and 15 are only represented in 'Seeing the bigger picture'. This is important for us to consider. Where else in the school/college curriculum are students given the space to explore their understanding and values linked to the principles within these goals? Perhaps an extension to this activity could be to map the learning aims from 'Seeing the bigger picture' to the 17 SDGs.

Progress towards Agenda 2030

In 2023, the UN and the UK governments acknowledged that progress in achieving Agenda 2030 is stalling.[9] The global pandemic and international conflict have affected sustainable development. Quite rightly this progress report focuses on the UK's global aid; however, national progress should also be monitored as we all work together to achieve economic, social and environmental sustainable development across the UK.

The young people we are supporting now will be the higher education students and early career professionals of the future. Understanding local, national and international politics will help make them become productive members of society and agents of change.

Using the SDGs to transform career development work

We know that good career education can lead to positive outcomes for students. Can careers education also save the planet? Using the SDGs within careers education can be transformative – transforming how young people think about their careers and future work and how they can make the world a better place.

Candy Ho holds the position of Chancellor's Research Chair at Kwantlen Polytechnic University, Canada. An experienced career development practitioner, Candy advocates that we can use SDGs alongside career development work as acts of social justice, helping students discover their strengths and talents, enabling them to realise their purpose and how they can help their communities. Chapter 9 will explore how this can be adapted for use with students in the UK.

Conclusion

What will it be like if we achieve the SDGs? An end to poverty and hunger? Quality education and decent work that reduces inequality? Sustainable and safe urban areas with responsible production and consumption? All of this while also allowing the land and water to recover. Who wouldn't want that future?

The UN SDGs are important. They inform government policy, and there is a global commitment to work towards the 2030 Agenda for Sustainable Development. Those of us who support people with their career development can use the SDGs as a framework to scaffold the development and delivery of a programme. Considering the local, national and global impact of working towards, and achieving, the goals can help young people see how their values, interests and career ideas can help them find meaningful work that may also make the world a better place.

The next chapter will focus on how our career can be sustainable, encouraging young people to develop good career management skills. What 'career' means will be discussed, alongside how a person's values can shape their career. The chapter will look at skills through a 'green lens' and consider how lifelong learning will become more important in the workplace as technology develops and employers focus more on how their organisations can contribute to sustainable development.

 World of work example: The SDG5 Living Lab

Edinburgh Napier University and Women's Enterprise Scotland are working in partnership to promote gender equality by supporting women in business. Launched in 2024, the initiative provides networking and training opportunities for women in Scotland who want to set up their own business or develop their leadership skills.

www.napier.ac.uk/about-us/news/sdg5-living-lab-bright-red-triangle

How this is useful:

- Which organisations in your area have work-related initiatives that support women or marginalised groups?
- Invite representatives and former participants to speak to young people in school/college.

Chapter 2: The United Nations Sustainable Development Goals

 World of work example: Slaughter and May

Slaughter and May is a UK-based international law firm. It has identified six SDGs that align with the company's sustainable approach to business. The company has a set of values that show its commitment to clients, employees and society and clear objectives linked to people, the planet and peace and prosperity. www.slaughterandmay.com/our-firm/responsible-business/

How this is useful:

- Research companies that have put SDGs at the heart of their business strategies. Ask students to explore the company website; how is the company supporting the SDGs? What is the evidence? (See the UN Global Compact Network UK SDG Showcase report for examples.[10])
- Identify the key personnel in the company who support how the company works towards the SDGs. Can students find out anything about their career pathways? Can you invite them to talk with the students (in person or online)?
- Many companies have not actively embedded SDGs in the way they operate, yet their environmental, social and governance (ESG) strategies do support several SDGs. Can students map a company's ESG strategy to the SDGs?

 World of work example: Futerra

Futerra is a company focused on helping other businesses to change, make and train. www.wearefuterra.com/

There are three services that the company delivers:

- **Change Agency** – working with other businesses to help them develop their sustainability strategy and marketing campaigns;
- **Makes** – innovative sustainable products and services;
- **Academy** – delivers sustainability training to an organisation's staff.

How this is useful:

- Show the 'Make the Anthropocene Awesome' video to your students. How does it make them feel? Is it inspirational? If so, what does it inspire them to want to do in the short, medium and long term?
- Encourage students to explore the Change Agency section of the website. Which of the companies that Futerra have worked with do they recognise? How do they feel about their marketing campaigns? Had they thought before about how the company is trying to achieve its sustainability goals alongside its primary purpose?

- After students have looked at the Makes section of the website, challenge them to create their own 'hothouse' of innovation. What new products or services can they create? How is the product or service connected to the SDG?
- Futerra has worked with many global brands to train staff in sustainability basics. Which organisations are students aware of? Can they recognise any of the content covered in Futerra's training modules in the 'public face' of the organisation? (This may involve further research on those organisations' websites or social media.)

Chapter 3
A sustainable career

> Our working lives are long, let's help young people to have the skills to navigate this and have meaningful work and healthy jobs.

Introduction

Transitioning from education to employment can be exciting for some students and cause worry for others. There will be young people with whom you work who appear indifferent to this step and barely engage with the career education activities offered. Our job is to steady this transition – to encourage the excited to explore all opportunities so that they are making informed decisions, to help the nervous develop their self-efficacy and, perhaps most challenging of all, to help the demotivated to explore possible futures and begin to set goals.

How are people enabled to think about how their career is sustainable? How do we prepare our young people to have a working life of over 50 years? In this chapter we will focus on several definitions of career, including having a sustainable career, that will be useful for you to consider. The concept of 'green guidance' will also be introduced and how this can be used to inform the work you do with students and clients to help them develop good career management skills for successfully navigating their future work. The chapter will also discuss what decent and meaningful work is and why it is important for young people to consider this.

The way employers are working is changing as they respond to net zero and other sustainability targets, and so the examples and activities in this chapter and the case studies throughout the book will help you understand the implications of this on the workforce and how this relates to your students and clients. This chapter will also guide you in deconstructing the constructs of 'green guidance', 'green jobs' and 'green skills' so that you clearly understand the terms. You can then confidently help the young people you work with to see through the 'green noise' and know how to find out about the opportunities available to them and the skills and knowledge that will be helpful.

Definitions of career

Andrews and Hooley (2024) give a clear and holistic definition of career that you may have come across in *The Careers Leader Handbook*, our 'pathway through life, learning and work'.[1] Using this definition with students and clients is a simple way to help them to see that many factors affect our career, including other roles we have in life (such as family, caring responsibilities, hobbies and interests), and that learning doesn't stop when we leave formal education. A key theme throughout this book is that, whatever the work, we all need to keep learning, updating our skills and be willing to try new things.

As professionals, whether teachers or career practitioners, there are many definitions of career that we can draw on to inform our work. We may not use these terms with our students or clients, but the ideas that they convey can be used in discussions and activities, informing and empowering young people so that they enter the workplace with their eyes, and minds, open.

Protean career: Introduced in 1976 by Hall and Mirvis, the concept of the protean career has the individual designing and managing their career, rather than relying on the more traditional, linear progression offered by the company employing them. The individual is in control of their success, including defining what success means to them.[2]

Boundaryless career: Arthur and Rousseau (1996) take this further with the concept of the boundaryless career, when the individual moves from one organisation to another, not necessarily following a linear, upward trajectory.[3] This may be noticeable between the generations where expecting the 'job for life' is less likely than it may have been and individuals may have many jobs at one time that contribute to their career development.

Thirty years on, these definitions are almost prophetic and can underpin the way we prepare young people for their careers. Money and job status are not the main motivators or drivers for many people, and loyalty to one company seems less important. Worldwide events such as developments in technology, climate change, the pandemic and economic insecurity are factors affecting society, organisations and governments and how individuals think about their career. So, perhaps we need a description of a *sustainable career* that seems more current and appropriate for use with clients and young people.

Sustainable career: The following is adapted from the conceptual work of De Vos, Van der Heijden and Akkermans (2020):[4]

A sustainable career . . .

- involves agency, where the person has responsibility for their decisions, responding positively to external factors that may be out of their control;
- evolves in the social spaces that the person is in (home, societal, academic);
- involves the individual being productive and positively affecting the organisation;
- is cyclical and non-linear, affected by life events and changes;
- involves happiness, such as engagement, subjective success and fulfilling work;
- contributes to well-being, involving healthy working behaviours, minimal work stress and no burnout.

De Vos et al. identify tensions and barriers that we need to be aware of, to help young people have the skills to overcome obstacles, such as:

- Short-term factors versus long-term factors, such as rewards and workload.
- A person's avoidance of risk.
- Negative thinking that focuses on losses over gains.
- Tangible outcomes, such as salary and promotion, versus intangible outcomes, such as personal development.

Of course, a *sustainable career* does not occur in isolation, and we need to remember that the circumstances the individual is in and their psychological capital can greatly affect how they can manage their career.

Things to think about

- Does your careers education programme encourage discussion about what a sustainable career may look like and how to recognise this?
- Do teachers and other staff give opportunities for young people to develop the skills and types of capital to overcome barriers to progress and development such as those listed above?

Now that we have thought about how complex the topic of career can be, the next section will consider how to help young people have the tools to navigate this.

Further information about career theories can be found in:

- *Career Development: Theories in Practice* by Julia Yates, published by Trotman in 2024
- Career MarcR, https://marcr.net/

> **More information about: Skills versus capital**
>
> Skills are things a person can do well because they have an inclination towards them and have practised: intellectual (e.g. problem-solving and creativity), intrapersonal (e.g. adaptability and goal setting) and interpersonal (e.g. communication and teamwork). (For more information, see the section further on in this chapter.)
>
> A person's capital consists of 'assets' that increase their value/give them an advantage. Increasingly, in higher education, a person's capitals are referred to, as well as their skills. Examples include human (e.g. qualifications), social, cultural, psychological and economic. For more information specific to schools visit https://myfuture.edu.au/docs/default-source/insights/the_employability_capital_growth_model.pdf?sfvrsn=31b136db_1
>
>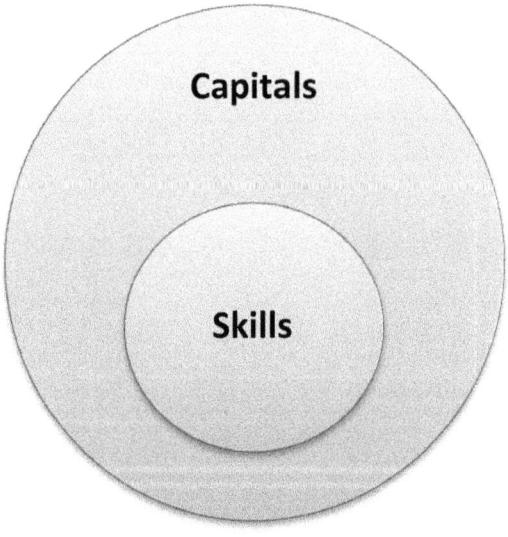

Career development

You may be a careers practitioner with a good understanding of career development and find my overview in this section simplistic. However, if you are a teacher or careers leader reading this book with little background knowledge, I hope you find this section on career development useful in the wider contexts of sustainability and sustainable careers.

The conversations around *employability* and *skills* are huge in schools and colleges in the UK. But for at least two decades, many career professionals have also been using the construct *career adaptability*, that is, 'the readiness to cope with the predictable tasks of preparing for and participating in the work role and with the unpredictable adjustments prompted by changes in work and working conditions'.[5]

In a nutshell, to be able to adapt, a person requires the following competencies: concern, control, curiosity, confidence and, more recently added, commitment.[6] The following gives a brief description of each competency. The development of these for an individual is ongoing, so think about how you could provide opportunities for students (or clients) to grow.

1. **Concern:** How much does your young person think about their future? Are they aware of issues such as when to leave full-time education, how to find work and what future learning they may need?

2. **Control:** Does the young person need prompting with every step, or are they more proactive? Are they able to set goals and be disciplined and organised to try and achieve them? Can they reflect on their progress and adjust plans accordingly?

3. **Curiosity:** Do they ask questions such as: 'What could I do?' 'How can I find out more about . . .?' 'How can I contribute to solving this problem?' How much exploration of their options for future transitions do they do?

4. **Confidence:** Does the young person have the self-efficacy (belief) that they can achieve their goals?

5. **Commitment:** In this context, commitment means are they able to develop persistence by experimenting with, and committing to, new activities so that they increase their chances of developing opportunities.

If young people develop these competencies then they are on the way to having good career management skills (CMS). From Skills Development Scotland, CMS are:[7]

- **Self:** Competencies that enable individuals to develop their sense of self within society.
- **Strengths:** Competencies that enable individuals to acquire and build on their strengths and to pursue rewarding learning and work opportunities.

- **Horizons:** Competencies that enable individuals to visualise, plan and achieve their career aspirations throughout life.
- **Networks:** Competencies that enable individuals to develop relationships and networks of support.

The following practical details can be added to this:

- Know *how to research* local and national job and education opportunities. (Teach research skills, such as starting with a clearly defined research question.)
- Understand how to apply for a job or course and how to navigate the selection and interview process. (Give opportunities to practice a variety of types of application and interview processes.)
- Understand the value of continuous professional development and lifelong learning, in all areas of life, after formal education is finished. (Through vicarious experiences: hear *relatable* career stories about learning and career progression.)

Hopefully, the information in this section will give ideas and practical suggestions to help your students and clients to be adaptable and agile so that they can thrive during their working lives. De Vos et al. argue that career development is an ongoing process affected by many factors, but that if we get it right, as professionals, we can move on from just impact *on* the individual's career towards the impact *of* careers on the environment and society. This links with the ideas introduced in chapters 1 and 2. The push for net zero and nature restoration is happening, and young people *will* be part of this. How much they contribute will depend on their interests and engagement, and as teachers and career professionals we can help students explore how they can use their career to make the world a better place.

Things to think about

- Does your careers education programme allow opportunities for students to develop the competencies listed in this section? (Note: students don't need to know these terms.)
- Do teachers and other staff understand why these competencies are important, and how they can help their students develop these in subject lessons? (Note: staff should be able to recognise these developing competencies in their students.)

Learning is lifelong

Research by public opinion specialists IPSOS shows that half of 24–34-year-olds expect to be in the same organisation when they retire.[8] That means half are expecting to change employer.

Many people tend not to actively consider their career planning until a 'driver' forces them to reconsider their job. Why do people look for a new job? According to IPSOS research, men tend to be *pulled* by positive factors, such as more pay or job status, and women tend to be *pushed* by negative factors, such as work culture or relationships.[8] In reality, a person's gender should not dictate the type of factor that will affect them; however, many studies show that women have lower self-perceived employability than men. As well as preparing people for their first job, schools and colleges can help all students explore the reasons people may look for new employment.

Young people in their early careers want to know about new job opportunities and want advice about how they can use their skills in different jobs. However, awareness and use of formal career advice for those in employment is low. This will probably need to be paid for once a person has left full-time education. We can help young people understand how beneficial a career professional can be, *at any time in their lives*, to help increase motivation and confidence and, therefore most importantly, life satisfaction.

Encouraging ongoing career planning from an early age can help young people understand the value of taking advantage of new learning and training opportunities and engaging with professional career guidance. Did you know that many universities offer career support to their alumni and local Further Education colleges usually offer prospective adult learners career advice?

Learning is also 'life-wide'; that is, our personal development occurs in both our home and social life.

Things to think about

- Are young people provided with the skills to remain engaged in meaningful work with a single employer? (To learn about networking, collaboration and continuous professional development.)
- Are young people equipped with the self-efficacy and agency to effectively look for new job opportunities? (For example, seeking professional help to understand how their skills are transferrable.)

> **Interesting fact**
>
> The pandemic caused some people to re-evaluate their lives, and the phenomenon of the 'great resignation' was observed. To mitigate this, many organisations are creating a continuous learning culture to ensure a sustainable workforce.
>
> www.computerweekly.com/feature/How-to-create-a-sustainable-continuous-learning-culture

Decent work

What makes a job a decent one? How do we prepare our young people to expect, and accept, decent work?

The International Labour Organization's (ILO's) website has a good overview of the concept of decent work and a short video that can be shared with students.[9]

> Decent work sums up the aspirations of people in their working lives. It involves opportunities for work that is productive and delivers a fair income, security in the workplace and social protection for all, better prospects for personal development and social integration, freedom for people to express their concerns, organize and participate in the decisions that affect their lives and equality of opportunity and treatment for all women and men.[9]

This definition and video are for a global audience, and while this may be received well by some students, we will need to make this relevant to those young people who are more concerned about their future and immediate problems.

We can have different types of jobs at different stages of our lives. The benefits of working on the shop floor or waiting on tables may be perfect for a young person developing their interpersonal skills, but will this job provide decent work as they transition into adulthood and take on new life roles and responsibilities? Helping young people to explore careers and pay progression to find out if that type of work will meet their needs, as they age, is important.

Young people should be made aware of 'precarious work'; that is, work which may have a zero-hours contract, is insecure and has limited progression opportunities. The Scottish government commissioned research about young people and precarious work, and this highlights the benefits and risks of such work.[10] The report concludes that many young people lack knowledge about what type of work is classed as precarious. The report also found that those young people in precarious work were less likely to be satisfied with their job, for example, due to lack of notice about being required, or not, to work.

See chapter 9 to find out about Greater Manchester's Good Employment Charter and how you can use this in your careers education programme.

Things to think about

- Are young people encouraged to think about how the type of work they have may change as they age?
- Does your careers programme include an exploration of career and pay progression?
- Do young people have the opportunity to learn about their employment rights?

Work and well-being

This leads us to consider health and well-being and the work/life balance. Work should not make us ill. Our work should enhance the quality of our lives, for example, providing an income to live well, providing social contact and giving us a sense of purpose in doing something worthwhile. 'Healthy jobs' can even improve retention for a company and help people to work for longer. (Very important, as the retirement age is rising for each generation!) The three indicators of a sustainable career are health, happiness and productivity, although we may not have all at any one time.[4]

It is important for young people to have agency and to make good career decisions for themselves. Many factors interact to affect our physical and mental health and work is one of them. The market researcher Gallup studies *career well-being* and defines it as 'you like what you do every day'.[11]

If we can help young people to be aware of and develop healthy work behaviours, it may reduce their susceptibility to work-related stress and burnout. These positive behaviours include:

- setting boundaries (very important with hybrid working);
- finding good role models (who can be supportive and mentor career progression planning);
- using emotional intelligence (to be able to reflect on their behaviour and develop positive working relationships).

A good employer prevents situations that can lead to work stress and can respond to and support an employee if they begin to suffer work stress. For example, an employer should not allow someone to return to the same job, unless some form of constructive intervention has taken place. The charity Mental Health UK helps people to recognise the signs of work stress and so prevent burnout. Signs include:

- being at work but not very productive;
- feeling helpless, trapped or defeated;
- frequent absence from work.

As employees, if we get this right and have career well-being, it can increase our life and job satisfaction. Therefore, having conversations with young people about developing behaviours for personal growth and having a sustainable career is a key part of their career education, helping them to have the skills to address the challenges they will face and leverage the opportunities that may come before them.

De Vos et al. highlight that our careers are changing, becoming longer and less predictable. Lifelong learning and upskilling are increasingly more important, and talent will be as desirable as qualifications for employers. However, some organisations are clinging on to the old views of a career, such as matching prospective employees with a job description, and the over-reliance of the pay ladder as a motivator. The boundaries between home and work are blurred, and the personal meaning of a *successful career* is changing as people have different priorities at different stages of their life (i.e. money, progression, job satisfaction, work-life balance). Although more of us will take ownership of our careers and expect some autonomy with selecting professional development, there are limits to an individual's agency as their social environment and time have an impact on a person's career.[4] (Makes you think about protean and boundaryless career definitions from the 20th century, doesn't it?)

Things to think about

- How do we help students to find out about career well-being with prospective employers? What research they can do and what questions can they ask?
- Give young people the opportunity to explore what having a successful career means to them. Do they imagine their definition will be the same at different stages in their life?

Green guidance

As mentioned in this chapter, good career guidance can help to change the world for the better. According to the Green Guidance website,

> Green guidance is a development of career guidance in which people are supported to make their education, training and employment choices with an awareness of and concern about the climate crisis and other environmental issues. Green guidance is not just about directing workers into a small sub-set of 'sustainable' industries, rather it is about helping people to understand the environmental impacts of their working lives and develop more positive and sustainable ways forward.[12]

Green guidance isn't about persuading young people to become engineers and build wind turbines! Lawyers, accountants, marketing specialists, hospitality and retail workers, charity workers, teachers and healthcare professionals – just about every job has a part to play in social justice, climate control, nature restoration and improving the world for future generations. Many people want to know that their job isn't negatively affecting society or the environment and may, in fact, be doing some good.

If a person's values are congruent with their employer's values, they are more likely to experience decent work, use their skills, feel valued and have a sense of belonging.

Things to think about

- Explore work values with young people. (For examples of how to do this, see *STEM Careers*, 2nd edition, Trotman.) Following this, encourage them to consider how *their* work values may link to their values about society and the environment.
- Explore the Sustainable Development Goals (SDGs). (See chapters 2 and 9 for suggested activities.) Following this, encourage young people to consider which SDGs they think are important and which industries/sectors this goal is linked to.

In chapter 9 there is a more detailed discussion about how you can use environmentally sustainable career guidance as a framework for your school/college programme.

Skills

The UK does not have a common skills taxonomy for all the skills that employers require of their employees. So, how can we teach young people about the skills they need if the topic is muddied with different lists? You may have come across organisations and programmes that attempt to give a clear, manageable list of (non-qualification) skills that education can help students develop. In *STEM Careers* (2nd edition), the debate is simplified by introducing the idea that all skills can be put into one of three categories:

1. **Intellectual:** Skills linked to your knowledge and how you perform tasks and solve problems.
2. **Intrapersonal:** Skills linked to how you manage your emotions and performance at work (self-awareness).
3. **Interpersonal:** Skills linked to how you work with other people, both within your organisation and externally.

The climate emergency and the technological revolution are causing the world of work to change, and the mismatch between the skills employers require and those young people (and the wider workforce) have is becoming greater.[13]

Things to think about

- How does your organisation frame the skills discussion with young people?
- Is the language used consistent across curriculum areas?

More information about: Skills England

In 2024, the new Labour government created Skills England, to work in partnership with Combined Authorities, industry and post-16 training providers (including colleges and schools with 6th forms) to ensure the workforce has the skills required for the country's economic growth.

The Unit for Future Skills, an analytical and research organisation, is now part of Skills England. The work of the Institute for Apprenticeships and Technical Education (IfATE) will transfer to Skills England.

Chapter 3: A Sustainable Career

> In the first few months of its inception, Skills England has:
>
> - produced a Local Skills Dashboard that provides a range of local labour market information (LMI) data including post-16 destination, local skills and employment projections. https://department-for-education.shinyapps.io/local-skills-dashboard/
> - produced an Occupation in Demand index. https://explore-education-statistics.service.gov.uk/find-statistics/occupations-in-demand/2024
>
> These tools provide up-to-date LMI that a teacher could use in their lessons or careers adviser could use during guidance meetings.
>
> Skills England aims to devolve decisions about skills training to the Combined Authorities. They also intend to consult employers and sector organisations for their views on what priority skills training is required, accessible via the Growth and Skills Levy.
>
> For more information visit www.gov.uk/government/collections/skills-england.

Green skills – a big idea

If you have turned to this section looking for a list you can share with colleagues, you may be disappointed!

According to the UK Parliament briefing paper from January 2024, green skills can be defined as 'the knowledge, abilities, values and attitudes needed to live in, develop and support a society which reduces the impact of human activity on the environment'.[13] Although green skills are usually associated with green jobs (see overleaf), it is acknowledged that, to various extents, all jobs will require green skills as the country moves towards net zero.

Chapter 1 discussed the jingle-jangle of terms. This is worth thinking about for a moment. Different organisations have different understandings of what green skills mean. In the energy sector, this is likely to mean engineering and technical skills. In hospitality and retail, green skills may include sourcing suppliers that reduce the food miles and packaging that is environmentally sustainable. In management, green skills may include collaboration and partnership working, while in business support, the green skills desirable may be data management and information handling.

Perhaps a way to help us think of whether a skill is green or not is to use the definition above as a 'green lens' to look through when considering any skill, that is, can using that skill 'develop and support a society which reduces the impact of human activity on the environment'?

In the drive for the UK to reach net zero by 2050 (see chapter 1 for more information), EVERY job has a part to play. That means EVERY person has to take action, in all parts of their life – home, education, work and leisure. And so EVERYONE needs 'green skills'.

> **World of work example: Bootcamps in sustainability**
>
> Some training providers offer 'Skills Bootcamps in Sustainability', helping participants develop a sustainability mindset to have the skills to create a sustainability transformation plan for their organisation. There can also be the possibility of gaining accreditation in nationally recognised awards.
>
> **How this is useful:**
>
> Visit your local training providers' websites to see if they offer such programmes. Could they be adapted for your students? For an example, visit https://adult.activatelearning.ac.uk/skills-bootcamp-in-sustainability/.
>
> (See chapter 7 for more information about qualifications.)

The Institute for Employment Research (IER) at Warwick University is researching the skills required 'to deliver a digital and green future for industry 5.0'.[14] (Industry 5.0 is a relatively new concept where digital and industrial developments are used to tackle environmental and societal issues.) This is a four-year project, due to finish in 2026, but at the NICEC conference on Sustainability and Careers in 2024, project lead Professor Christopher Warhurst summarised some of the findings so far:

1. **Robots are not taking over!** Jobs in the future will be more complicated and require more skills. Positives are that workers will have more autonomy, higher pay and jobs will be more secure. Some new jobs will appear, some will disappear but the majority will just have some change, that is, not many new green jobs but existing jobs 'greening' (i.e. upskilling).

2. **The green revolution is happening.** From producing clean energy to nature restoration and working more sustainably, the extent and demand for green jobs are rising. (See below for more information about green jobs.)

3. **There are skills shortages.** This is complicated as the supply of workers actually outstrips demand, but why don't they have the skills the employers want? And why aren't employers making better use of the workers they have? Upskilling and retraining will be increasingly part of our careers, and instilling the need for continuous professional development in our students is vital.

Things to think about

- How can you reframe 'skills' as 'green skills' in your school/college?
- Give young people the opportunity to explore their existing skills framework through a 'green lens'.

Green jobs

Green jobs specifically focus on improving the environmental outcomes for a company, organisation or society. Research commissioned by Skills Development Scotland (SDS) has identified three types of green jobs:[15]

1. **Green new and emerging:** Such as involved in clean energy and renewables, for example, solar system technician and small module reactor designer. (Note, there are not as many of these jobs as people may think!)

2. **Green enhanced:** Existing jobs that use new skills and knowledge, for example, environmental lawyer and architect. (Note, these types of jobs are experiencing the greatest demand by employers.)

3. **Green increased demand:** The job hasn't changed, but the work context has, for example, engineering and trade skills, such as electricians. (Note, these roles are traditionally dominated by men.)

Chapter 4 will focus on each type of green job, giving examples of specific roles and sectors they can be found in.

Reports from the UK Parliament and Nesta specifically focus on the types of green skills required to get us to net zero, and, currently, the skills shortage is a barrier to the UK achieving this.[13,16] Key sectors, such as energy and construction, tend to have an ageing workforce, so all stakeholders understand the need to attract younger, more diverse employees and upskill the existing workforce. Read case study 1 to find out how Balfour Beatty is approaching this. Nesta's research showed that many young people are willing to train for 'green jobs' and existing employees are willing to upskill, but the financial implication of further study can be a barrier. This is something that the UK government and devolved nations, along with commercial partners, will need to address.

Sustainable Careers

Things to think about

- Young people are concerned about the impact of artificial intelligence (AI) on their jobs,[17] therefore reduce their fears by helping students explore how AI and automation can be useful tools in the workplace.
- Know your local labour market. Who are the local employers of the three types of green jobs?

Sustainability and the workforce

Although this book is written for adults who support young people with their career learning, there are issues that employers must navigate that are worth being aware of.

- A company must plan its future workforce. Are they upskilling employees and proactive about the succession of the workforce?
- Retention of employees and their health and well-being. Are they creating a positive culture and fostering a sense of belonging, especially in recruits?
- What place does environmental, social and governance (ESG) have in the organisation? How is this related to their output? How are ESG commitments met?

Conclusion

This chapter has introduced different definitions of a career, leading us to consider what a *sustainable career* is and what competencies are required to successfully manage one.

Everyone should strive to have a sustainable career that enables growth, contentment and security. We can help young people explore their values and skills so that they can develop their sense of agency and self-efficacy, enabling the individual to feel they have control over their future working lives.

Young people may be entering a workplace that is different to anything they have experienced so far. The lure of hybrid working may seem to offer flexibility, but in reality, many companies are trying to get employees back in the office and young people may not understand the positives and negatives of working from home.

In the drive towards net zero and other SDGs, employers are seeking different skills in the workforce that may be termed green skills. There is the potential for female workers and young people to be left behind in the green work revolution, as trades traditionally followed by men take advantage of the increased demand. Employers value their existing staff, and training/upskilling opportunities may be offered to them over new apprentices. Therefore, we must ensure that all young people have information about and access to vocational education and training.

Research has shown that green jobs fall into three categories: new and emerging jobs, enhanced jobs that already exist and existing jobs that are in increased demand. The following three chapters will explore these further. Chapter 4 will examine the three types of green jobs in further detail. In chapter 5, sectors that directly impact sustainable development will be discussed, while chapter 6 will explore how other sectors are working more sustainably.

Chapter 4
Careers in sustainability (types of green jobs)

> This chapter is probably the reason why you picked up this book!

Introduction

As introduced in chapter 3, research carried out by the Warwick Institute for Employment Research examining jobs in Scotland found three types of green job.[1] Although this report focused on Scotland, the categories of jobs apply across the UK and provide a useful framework to explore green jobs and labour market information with young people. However, do bear in mind that the Green Jobs Taskforce states that creating a single definition for a 'green job' is a complex task.[2]

The three types of green jobs identified are:

1. **Green new and emerging:** Unique work requiring new roles.
2. **Green enhanced:** Existing jobs that use new skills and knowledge.
3. **Green increased demand:** The job hasn't changed but the sector/industry has.

The demand for green jobs is growing; however, the report does point out that more evidence is required to understand exactly how the transition to net zero is affecting the demand for jobs and skills. This is backed up by the Office for National Statistics (ONS). The ONS defines green jobs as 'employment in an activity that contributes to protecting or restoring the environment, including those that mitigate or adapt to climate change'.[3] Their research shows that the number of green jobs is rising from an estimated 590,000 in 2021 to approximately 640,000 in 2022.[3] Importantly, one thing to be aware of is that most jobs in the UK do not fall into any of the three categories above. (See section 4 in this chapter for more information about sustainability in these jobs.)

So, where are these green jobs found? Work from the US Bureau of Labor Statistics found they are either:

A. Jobs in businesses that produce goods or provide services that benefit the environment or conserve natural resources.

or

B. Jobs in which workers' duties involve making their organisation's production processes more environmentally friendly or using fewer natural resources.[4]

Things to think about

- For any company, consider if it produces goods or offers a service.
- Do those goods or services directly benefit the environment or conserve natural resources?
- If the answer is no, is the company actively striving to be more environmentally friendly or use fewer natural resources in its production processes?

The next part of this chapter will focus on the three types of green jobs and examples of occupations. Examples of sectors and industries where the three types of jobs can be found and are crucial to the UK meeting its net zero targets are listed below (these will be discussed in greater detail in chapters 5 and 6):[2]

- Low-carbon energy production (e.g. solar, hydrogen, wind, hydropower).
- Industrial decarbonisation of businesses, including carbon capture.
- Transport (e.g. aviation, maritime, low-emission vehicles).
- Nature restoration, conservation and waste management.
- Climate adaptation (e.g. retrofitting buildings, flood defences).
- Science and innovation, including green finance, the circular economy and energy storage.

All businesses, whether large or small, have a role to play in reducing energy consumption and CO_2 emissions. Therefore, this chapter will also include a review of how more traditional jobs have changed as all sectors work towards achieving net zero by 2050. You can read more about Balfour Beatty's approach to sustainability in case study 1; how a sustainability manager is encouraging staff and students to be more sustainable in case study 2; how a start-up company is working sustainably in case study 3; and how a school is adapting how it operates in case study 4.

1. New green and energy occupations

The impact of green economy activities and technologies creates the need for unique work and worker requirements, which results in the generation of new occupations. These new occupations can be entirely novel or 'born' from an existing occupation.[1]

Most of the new and emerging jobs are for professionals, such as engineers, in sectors associated directly with benefitting the environment or conserving natural resources, such as renewable energy and waste treatment. Take time to find out about your local labour market, as there are pockets around the UK where demand for new and emerging green jobs is concentrated, for example, in southwest Scotland.[1]

Examples of new green and energy occupations include:

- Solar engineer;
- Energy engineer;
- Energy manager;
- Energy efficiency specialist;
- Sustainability consultant;
- Sustainability site manager;
- Project engineer;
- Civil engineer;
- Electrical engineer;
- Renewable energy analyst;
- Science technician;
- Wind turbine engineer.

People in occupations such as those listed above are probably employed in industries providing energy-efficient products, waste management, low-carbon transport, renewable energy and environmental services.[3] One thing worth thinking about is that businesses operating in these industries are probably growing and therefore developing *all* of their workforce, not just the specific green occupations. You can help young people explore other opportunities in these growing companies, such as in marketing, business support and human resources.

You can read more about how a sustainability manager at a university is encouraging staff and students to be more sustainable in case study 2, in chapter 7.

> **World of work example: Renewable energy analyst**
>
> Go Construct provides information and resources about careers in the construction sector. Their 'What jobs are right for me?' section provides information about specific jobs, skills required, salary and training routes. One example of such a job is a renewable energy analyst: www.goconstruct.org/construction-careers/what-jobs-are-right-for-me/renewable-energy-analyst/.
>
> **How this is useful:**
>
> Give students time to explore this job information from the Go Construct website. Show young people how to research if a job is in demand: use the term 'renewable energy analyst' to search for current job opportunities. Are there any in your area? What other terms are used to describe this occupation?

2. Green enhanced

> *The impact of green economy activities and technologies can result in significant change to the work and worker requirements of existing occupations. This impact may result in an increase in demand for these occupations. The essential purposes of the occupation remain the same but tasks, skills, knowledge and external elements, such as credentials, have been altered.*[1]

This type of green job is dominated by managerial positions and professional roles that require education and training. They can be found in companies whose primary role is to contribute to net zero or nature restoration or in more traditional organisations with clear environmental, sustainability strategies.

Examples of green-enhanced occupations include:

- Architect;
- Town planner;
- Logistics manager;
- Sales (e.g. solar panels);
- Retail manager;

- Event manager;
- Software developer;
- Heat pump engineer;
- Legal (solicitor and lawyer);
- Financial (accountant and analyst);
- Conservationist;
- Ecologist.

It's worth remembering that these occupations are not new (architects have been around since civilisations developed!). Also consider that these occupations have always been at the forefront of technological and scientific developments, learning new skills as new materials became available. Think about how construction has changed during the last 2,000 years!

In chapter 6 you can read how Balfour Beatty is changing the mindset of its employees, helping all areas of the company to meet their sustainability targets.

 World of work example: Heat pump engineers

Heat pump engineers install and service zero-carbon central heating and hot water systems in homes and businesses. Entry into this role could be via training to be a plumber, heating and ventilation engineer or gas service technician, followed by an additional short course. Alternatively, there is a Level 3 Advanced Apprenticeship to become a low-carbon heating technician.

For more information visit: https://nationalcareers.service.gov.uk/job-profiles/heat-pump-engineer.

How this is useful:

Explore the local labour market. What local companies offer installation and servicing of zero-carbon central heating and hot water systems? What local training is available, and is this through the company or an education provider?

> **World of work example: Green Finance Institute**
>
> Watch this video that explains the importance of incorporating sustainability education into finance professionals' training: https://youtu.be/RPpQRrPwaml?list=TLGG93oJPNN-ZyQwMzA5MjAyNA.
>
> And you can find more information about the Sustainable Finance Education Charter at:
>
> www.greenfinanceinstitute.com/home/resources/education-charter/.
>
> **How this is useful:**
>
> Use this as an example for young people who already have a career profession in mind. They can explore the traditional training pathways AND the new learning associated with sustainable development.

3. Green increased demand occupations

The impact of green economy activities and technologies can increase employment demand for some existing occupations. However, this impact does not entail significant changes in the work and worker requirements of the occupation. The work context may change but the tasks do not.[1]

The Skills Development report about green jobs uses the ONS classification of occupations, and this type of green job is dominated by:[1,3]

- *elementary occupations* that involve on-the-job training and may not require formal qualifications, such as production line worker, labourer, clerical and courier;
- *sales and customer service* roles;
- *skilled trades*, such as joiner, electrician, horticulturist, caterer and metal worker;
- *associate professional* jobs that require formal qualifications and training, such as IT, architectural and scientific technicians;
- *process, plant and machine operatives* that require formal training, including specialist vehicle drivers such as HGV.

Looking at the quote above, many of these roles may not appear to be directly linked to sustainability, but consider how a green organisation or initiative (i.e. an organisation whose primary purpose is to contribute towards low-carbon/renewable energy or nature restoration) can directly affect employment at a local level. This will include everything from office staff, maintenance, factory floor and distribution.

Chapter 4: Careers in Sustainability (Types of Green Jobs)

Things to think about

- Which type of green job is it? How do students (and ourselves) decide? Have a look at specialist job websites such as www.greenjobs.co.uk/, https://jobs.ecocareers.org/ or www.environmentjob.co.uk/jobs.

Choose any job, look at the description and decide which category it best fits into:

1. New green and energy occupations (unique work in a new context)
2. Green enhanced (existing work but new knowledge needed for the context)
3. Green increased demand occupations (existing work and knowledge needed but in a new context)

- Encourage students to investigate **Green Jobs Tree**, an interactive platform for exploring macro sectors, industries, jobs and skills, based on the decision tree model, starting with the natural environment, built environment and green services: www.greenjobstree.eu/en/.

More information about: Green jobs – pay and gender

Research shows that green jobs are better paid than other jobs (average salary £29,673 compared to £23,837 in 2022) but men occupy most of the roles.[1] However, there are more women in type 2 (green enhanced) green jobs, and the gender gap in type 1 (new and emerging) is smaller than in type 3 (increased demand). As career professionals and teachers working with young people, we have a lot of work to do in raising the awareness of green jobs and challenging stereotypes, as 16–24-year-olds are under-represented across all types.

1. **Green new and emerging:** Unique work requiring new roles
2. **Green enhanced:** Existing jobs that use new skills and knowledge
3. **Green increased demand:** The job hasn't changed but the sector/industry has

4. And everyone else's job

This extra section has been added to reinforce the concept of working sustainably, introduced and discussed in the preceding chapters. To get the UK to net zero by 2050, *every* sector has to reduce its consumption of material resources, energy and water. That means *every* employee has a part to play.

World of work example: Your workplace

Take a moment to consider what decisions you and your students/clients make every day to help your workplace be more sustainable. Is your organisation encouraging or supporting this behaviour?

How this is useful:

Encourage conversations with young people and clients about:

- How to reduce energy usage at work.
- How to safely reduce water consumption in the workplace.
- How to reduce the use of materials and consumables without compromising the quality of the work output.

Case study 4, in chapter 9, describes how a school is adapting its operations and encouraging staff and students to be more aware of their impact on the environment.

Things to think about

Encourage young people and clients to use a reputable jobs website to search for jobs they are interested in.

- Is sustainability mentioned in the job description?
- Extending the research to the employer's website, is sustainability included in the company values?
- How might this information, or lack of it, be useful in the career decision-making process?

More information about: Types of businesses

It is worth taking a moment to consider the world of work and how we discuss this with students. Organisations either produce goods or offer a service, and involved in this will be the 'production process' (how the goods are made or the service delivered). The product or service could be for another business (often referred to as business-to-business, B2B) or for the public/consumer. From healthcare to higher education and manufacturing to media, this overview can be applied to all areas of the world of work.

Conclusion

Teachers can use information about the three types of green jobs in their discussions in the classroom. All subject areas, from creative arts to STEM and the humanities, will be contributing to the development of the future workforce, helping them to learn about emerging jobs and how existing ones linked to their subject are changing. Careers professionals can guide young people and clients about green jobs, as they explore their interests and research potential opportunities.

Creating new occupations and the 'greening' of existing ones is an ongoing process as new technologies and the green economy are developed to bring us to net zero, restore habitats and improve society for people. The language used in job descriptions is therefore also changing. We must encourage critical thinking when looking at job adverts with young people. Some companies may extol their green credentials when enticing new employees, so how can we enable job candidates to investigate this further to corroborate the facts? Encouraging young people to examine company websites, strategies and reports can empower them to prepare thoroughly for any potential job application.

Whether implicit or explicit, all jobs have some element of environmental, sustainable development or social goals. To prepare young people for this, encourage them to interrogate a job description to see if it fits into one of the three types of green jobs discussed in this chapter. (The 'Green Jobs' section on Careerpilot is a good place to start, https://careerpilot.org.uk/.) Added to this, in different regions of the UK there may be a concentration of one type of sector or industry. Following the local labour market can help future employees to make the most of upcoming opportunities. Chapter 5 will focus on the main sectors contributing to net zero and nature restoration, and chapter 6 will give information about exciting developments in other sectors, such as fashion and information technology.

Chapter 5
Sectors getting us to net zero

> Many sectors are innovating and pushing boundaries to protect the environment and reduce the levels of carbon dioxide in the atmosphere while providing the resources the country needs.

Introduction

The focus of the previous chapter is the different types of green jobs. The next two chapters will discuss the sectors in which these jobs can be found and give information about sustainability developments that will improve society, the environment and the economy.

This chapter is designed to give you an overview of how three large sectors are working to help the UK reach net zero, have a secure energy supply and mitigate against climate change and other environmental problems. These sectors are:

- energy;
- water and waste management;
- conservation.

Chapter 6 will focus on other sectors that are improving how they work while still delivering their primary aim of providing a service or product.

Net zero is discussed in chapter 1, but here is a little reminder about what it is and why it is important. Following the Paris Agreement of 2016, the UK pledged in law to reduce carbon emissions and reach net zero by 2050 (see the carbon budget information box).[1,2] This means that the total greenhouse gas emissions (such as carbon dioxide and methane) would equal their removal from the atmosphere. This should help to limit global warming, enabling recovery of the effects of climate change.

Success in meeting this goal will require the UK and home nation governments to set legally binding targets, public and private organisations to embrace the required changes to operations and individuals to understand the part they play, both within their work and home life. Chapter 3 discussed green skills, and chapter 4 explored three types of green jobs. Throughout the next two chapters, reference will be made to the employment needs of the sectors and signposting to further career information.

This field is changing rapidly; we have recently had a new UK government elected which is developing policies and changing targets. There are always new research data and technological developments. Both chapters will include signposting to lead you to reliable sector news and updates.

Economic opportunities

In February 2025, the Confederation of British Industry (CBI) and Energy and Climate Intelligence Unit released their joint report containing recent data about the UK's net zero economy and employment within sectors. Entitled *The Future is green: The economic opportunities brought by the UK's net zero economy,* headline statistics include the following:

- The net zero economy supports over 950,000 jobs, directly and indirectly (in the supply chain).
- There are over 15,000 net zero employers in the UK, with 95% classed as small to medium enterprises (SMEs).
- Renewable energy and waste management are the net zero sectors employing the most people.
- The largest regional contributors to the UK's net zero economy are South West England, Yorkshire and Humberside and the West Midlands.
- North East Scotland is a 'key net zero hotspot', adding 5.1% to the UK's net zero economy.

For more information, visit https://eciu.net/analysis/reports/2025/net-zero-economy-across-the-uk.

Energy

The UK's energy sector supports over 735,000 jobs – that's 1 in 50 jobs across England, Scotland, Wales and Northern Ireland.[3] It is predicted that by 2050, an extra 400,000 people will be needed to work in the energy sector.[4]

Energy is a big topic that includes electricity production for the nation, fuel required for transport and heating buildings. Your knowledge in this area might be good, but in case it's lacking, here is a brief overview that all UK students learn about in the science curriculum:

- Energy cannot be created or destroyed; it is converted from one form to another. For example, solar energy can be converted into electrical energy in solar panels.
- Most* electricity is produced in a power station when fuel is combusted, and the thermal energy released is used to heat liquid water into steam that turns a turbine, generating electricity.
- Turbines can also be turned by wind (wind power) and when liquid water flows (hydroelectric), removing the need to burn fuel.
- Nuclear fission energy can also be used to heat liquid water to steam and produce electricity via turbines.
- Electricity can be generated on a massive scale – such as in power stations and wind farms – and fed into the national grid or on a domestic scale for local use, such as solar panels and small-scale wind turbines.
- The national grid is a network of infrastructure that transports electricity across the UK from where it is produced to where it is consumed.

*For real-time data about the UK's electricity generation, see the National Grid section in this chapter.

If generating electricity directly involves combustion, then carbon dioxide is released. Traditionally, the UK relied on non-renewable energy resources such as coal, gas and oil (fossil fuels). The climate crisis and move to net zero requires more sustainable energy resources, such as wind, solar and nuclear. Decarbonisation of the energy industry in the UK is complex and is closely linked to energy security and a reduction in the reliance on imported energy sources.[5]

In July 2024, the new Labour government set up Great British Energy, a publicly owned, clean energy company that works with the Department for Energy Security and Net Zero. Its mission is to 'drive clean energy deployment to create jobs, boost energy independence, and ensure UK taxpayers, billpayers and communities reap the benefits of clean, secure, home-grown energy'.[5] The government has ambitious plans to decarbonise the UK's energy sector and have 'clean power' by 2030.[6] Energy UK, the trade association representing the sector, supports this ambition and has made recommendations to the government within its 'Mission Possible' report. You can track the government and sector's progress here: https://www.energy-uk.org.uk/insights/mission-possible-tracker/.

> **More information about: Carbon budgets**
>
> 'A carbon budget places a restriction on the total amount of greenhouse gases the UK can emit over a 5-year period. The UK is the first country to set legally binding carbon budgets.' (www.gov.uk/guidance/carbon-budgets)
>
> There are six five-year budgets and we are currently in the fourth carbon budget (2023–27), legislating that the UK will emit no greater than 1,950 million tonnes of carbon dioxide equivalent ($MtCO_2e$).*
>
> *$MtCO_2e$ standardises the measurement of other greenhouse gas emissions, such as methane and nitrous oxide, to the same global warming potential of carbon dioxide.
>
> | Carbon budget number | Time span | CO_2 budget cap (million tonnes of CO_2 equivalent) $MtCO_2e$ |
> |---|---|---|
> | First | 2008–12 | 3,018 |
> | Second | 2013–17 | 2,782 |
> | Third | 2018–22 | 2,544 |
> | Fourth | 2023–27 | 1,950 |
> | Fifth | 2028–32 | 1,725 |
> | Sixth | 2033–37 | 965 |
>
> The new government has announced that the sixth carbon budget will be exceeded, as the UK will aim for an 81% cut in emissions by 2035, rather than the proposed 78% cut (www.bbc.co.uk/news/articles/cx2ny8zndpxo).
>
> All sectors are involved, and a shortfall in one will need to be made up by reductions in another. Many companies operating in the UK have incorporated carbon budget targets into their strategies.
>
> See chapter 8 for a discussion about the ethical implications of carbon trading.

What is happening with fossil fuels?

The UK government is committed to decarbonising the UK power system, and more solar and wind farm infrastructure is required. However, as wind and solar sources are not reliable, the UK is not ready to completely move away from requiring fossil fuels for electricity production. This is for energy security reasons and to ensure the continuous supply of electricity when solar and wind sources are unreliable.[5] Therefore, we still rely on liquified natural gas (LNG) and gas-fired power stations, as gas is currently the greatest contributor to electricity production (see the section on hydrogen for more information).

Chapter 5: Sectors Getting Us to Net Zero

Visit Shell's website to read the company's views on the need for LNG: www.shell.com/what-we-do/oil-and-natural-gas/liquefied-natural-gas-lng.html.

From crude oil, we obtain fuels, such as petrol, diesel and kerosene, and raw materials for the manufacture of solvents, lubricants, detergents and plastics.[7] Researchers are investigating alternatives that can be produced from plant material, also known as bio-based compounds. This is an exciting area that will see collaboration between academics and private businesses involved in the production of solvents, lubricants, detergents and plastics.

At the time of writing the government is consulting to produce new environmental guidance for the North Sea gas and oil industries, ensuring climate obligations are met while also protecting jobs and economic growth. One initiative is to set up a 'skills passport' enabling people with experience in the oil and gas industry to move into employment within the offshore wind industry.[8]

Renewable energy

In April 2024, approximately 40% of the UK's energy production was from renewables. Three-quarters of this was used to generate electricity, and the remainder was used for transport and generating heat for homes and businesses.[9] Wind energy is the largest contributor, responsible for nearly 30% of renewable energy production. Cornwall generates the most electricity from solar energy, and the Orkney Islands generate the most electricity from onshore wind turbines. In the UK, Lancashire has the most offshore wind sites generating electricity and the Highlands of Scotland have the most hydroelectric schemes.[9]

It is worth remembering that renewable energy sources are indirectly linked to carbon production, as the processes involved in manufacturing equipment such as solar panels and wind turbines release CO_2. However, this can be offset by the carbon-free electricity they produce.

 Interesting fact

The Isle of Lewis in the Outer Hebrides is home to the largest community-owned wind farm in the UK, producing £900,000 net income for the community to support local people and projects: www.pointandsandwick.co.uk/about-us/our-wind-farm/.

> **Interesting fact**
>
> The Dogger Bank wind farm, off the northeast coast of England, is a joint venture between UK-based SSE Renewables and Norway-based Equinor and Vårgrønn. When complete it will be the world's largest offshore wind farm and provide enough electricity for 6 million homes. Community funds will be available during construction, supporting local STEM activities: https://doggerbank.com/.

Nuclear energy

Technically, energy from nuclear sources is not actually renewable as the raw material is used up and not easily replaced. Heat energy, generated by the breakdown of uranium (nuclear fission), is used in nuclear power stations. A lot is happening in the UK concerning the nuclear industry and sustainable energy supplies. This innovation and design will bring many job opportunities, from researchers to engineers:

1. The government is supporting the innovation and development of small modular reactors (SMRs). Six consortiums have been selected by the government to continue to develop their ideas to build small reactors that will generate 'clean' electricity at many locations across the UK, requiring less space than a traditional power plant. For more information visit: www.gov.uk/government/organisations/great-british-nuclear.

2. Efficient energy capture from fusion reactors is yet to be realised. It involves combining the nuclei of hydrogen to release energy. The UK Atomic Energy Authority (UKAEA) is a public body that researches fusion energy and related technologies. For more information visit: www.gov.uk/government/organisations/uk-atomic-energy-authority.

> **Interesting fact**
>
> Lots of uranium is found on Earth, and it is energy dense. A uranium fuel pellet is similar in size to one gummy bear sweet. The energy in a pellet is equivalent to one tonne of coal and would make enough electricity to power an electric car for 20,000 miles!

Chapter 5: Sectors Getting Us to Net Zero

 World of work example: Rolls-Royce SMR Ltd

This consortium of industry partners is working together to design and plan the building of SMRs to help secure the UK's long-term energy supply. Knowledge from the manufacturing, aerospace, nuclear, supply chain and logistics sectors is working together.

How this is useful:

Teachers of science and technology should keep up to date with developments and encourage discussion with students about this method of electricity production. What are the benefits to the regions that would have an SMR? What considerations will SMR companies need to have with local communities?

www.rolls-royce-smr.com

Share the story about how a social media influencer is helping people to learn about nuclear energy: www.ted.com/talks/isabelle_boemeke_nuclear_power_is_our_best_hope_to_ditch_fossil_fuels.

For more information about employment in the nuclear sector visit: https://nuclearskillsdeliverygroup.com/wp-content/uploads/2024/05/NSDG-National-Nuclear-Strategic-Plan-For-Skills.pdf.

Find out about career opportunities and work placements within the UKAEA and partner organisations at: https://careers.ukaea.uk/early-careers/placements-and-work-experience/.

Hydrogen

Hydrogen will play an important part in the UK's low-carbon energy generation.

Hydrogen can be manufactured using electrolysis when electricity is used to break down water into hydrogen and oxygen. This is called 'green hydrogen' if the electricity used is from a renewable source. Heating natural gas, a fossil fuel, with steam can also form (blue) hydrogen, but the carbon waste needs to be captured (see overleaf).[10]

This is quite a complex industry, as electricity is needed to manufacture hydrogen. The electricity produced from wind and solar energy cannot be stored, so excess can be used to make hydrogen. The beauty is that this hydrogen can be transported to where it is required or compressed and stored.

When electricity is needed, the hydrogen enters a fuel cell where it reacts with oxygen, generating electricity. This electricity can be used for heating and to power homes and industry. There is a lot of research and development regarding manufacturing hydrogen, developing the network of pipes to transport hydrogen and the technology in buildings and vehicles to use hydrogen as a fuel. The UK government is committed to backing hydrogen energy projects, and this will lead to increased jobs across the UK.[10,11,12]

 World of work example: Hynet North West

This partnership, based in North West England and North Wales, provides the infrastructure to produce, transport and store low-carbon hydrogen (https://hynet.co.uk/). This will help local industries to decarbonise, as they use hydrogen to power their processes, instead of electricity made from fossil fuels.

How this is useful:

Explore the website – who are the industry partners? Do they make products that young people use? What are the career opportunities? Is there a similar consortium in your region?

More information about: Carbon capture, utilisation and storage (CCUS)

CCUS involves the capture of waste carbon dioxide (CO_2) gas from power stations and industrial processes. The CO_2 can be used in the manufacture of fertilisers, and research has been carried out to use the captured CO_2 in building materials and synthetic fuel production. Storage of captured CO_2 in the UK would potentially be deep in the rocks below the North and Irish Seas. For more information visit the International Energy Agency (IEA) website. This global organisation works with governments and industry to shape a secure and sustainable energy future for all: www.iea.org/energy-system/carbon-capture-utilisation-and-storage.

The CCUS information video from the Carbon Capture and Storage Association can help students learn more about this developing area. Facilitate a discussion about the potential jobs involved in CCUS. What examples would be in each type of green job (see chapter 4 for explanation)?

1. New green and energy occupations
2. Green enhanced
3. Green increased demand occupations

www.bing.com/videos/riverview/relatedvideo?q=CCUS+in+the+uk&mid=7EEE6CF09FFBD9D59B0E7EEE6CF09FFBD9D59B0E&FORM=VIRE

Chapter 5: Sectors Getting Us to Net Zero

The 'National Grid'

We think of the 'national grid' as the way electricity is distributed across the UK, from where it is generated to where it is used. The company National Grid is actually just one of the distributors in the UK, operating in the Midlands, South West England and South Wales. Another example is Northern PowerGrid, distributing in the North East, Yorkshire and northern Lincolnshire. All of the distributors are overseen by the National Energy System Operator (NESO) for Great Britain: www.neso.energy.

Live data is available to see real-time reporting on the sources of our electricity. Here are three sites that display the data in a user-friendly format:

- www.energydashboard.co.uk/live
- https://grid.iamkate.com/
- www.energydashboard.co.uk/live

Visit the NESO website and the individual distributor websites for information about careers that will help you to learn about the types of jobs in demand.

Electricity providers

The provider (supplier) buys energy from the producers and sells it to households, businesses and other users. This is a competitive market; companies often merge and restructure, and the energy crisis has caused many suppliers to go out of business. The market is therefore regulated, and prices are capped by the government (Ofgem).[13]

World of work example: Octopus Energy

Octopus Energy, launched in 2016 by tech entrepreneur Greg Jackson, has been disrupting the energy market during the last decade. Rooted in fair pricing, customer care and investments in green energy, the company has become one of the UK's largest suppliers. The Octopus account dashboard was built by the company's apprentices. They are championing new technology too, training thousands of engineers to install heat pumps and developing new information technology platforms to increase efficiency: https://octopus.energy/.

How this is useful:

Talk to young people about how entrepreneurs and disruptors are finding new solutions to old problems. See chapter 8 for more information about entrepreneurs and disruptors.

See more about training for heat pump engineers in chapter 4.

57

More information about: Information technology

Society has come to rely on information technology, and the government has classified data centres as 'critical national infrastructure'.[14] Data centres are the physical locations of the computers that power artificial intelligence applications, cloud storage, data processing and streaming. Companies such as Amazon and Google are building their own sites and this investment is leading to job growth. Google even has plans to power its sites using SMRs. The energy and water consumption to power and cool the sites is large and while this is of environmental concern, research and development are leading to solutions, such as supplying the heat to local communities.[14,15]

Things to think about

Research has shown that a search using ChatGPT rather than a traditional search engine can use up to 40 times more electricity, with image creator services using even more! Listen to this episode of The Artificial Human podcast for more information. Promote discussions with young people about how they can sensibly use language models such as ChatGPT: www.bbc.co.uk/sounds/play/m00208g4?partner=uk.co.bbc&origin=share-mobile.

Jobs in the energy sector

So what types of jobs does the energy sector require? According to National Grid, the energy sector needs civil, mechanical and electrical engineers, data analysts, machine learning experts and skilled tradespeople. There will also be new roles linked to electric vehicles, hydrogen and carbon capture technology.[4] To share information about early career opportunities and training schemes with young people, visit the websites of companies in the energy sector to see examples of roles available.

Keep up to date with news and developments in the UK's energy sector (www.energy-uk.org.uk/) and updates from the government's Department for Energy Security and Net Zero: www.gov.uk/government/organisations/department-for-energy-security-and-net-zero.

Chapter 5: Sectors Getting Us to Net Zero

 World of work example: Siemens Energy

Global company Siemens Energy is involved in developing the technology required for energy production and transferring and storing electricity. It is also involved in helping organisations electrify their industrial processes.

How this is useful:

There are blogs and career stories that you can share with young people, including 'We do the maths for sustainability':

www.siemens-energy.com/global/en/home/careers/working-at-siemens-energy-html.

Water and waste management

Providing water and processing waste are closely linked with the environment. Therefore, for this book, these industries have been included in this chapter as their activities directly affect the quality of our water systems, the air and the land. Significant factors affecting the water industry's move to net zero and nature restoration will be discussed first, followed by the developments in the management of other household and industrial waste. Finally, the concept of the circular economy will be introduced.

The water industry

The UK water industry is made up of Scottish Water, Northern Ireland Water and many companies across England and Wales that provide drinking water and process wastewater in their area. Unlike energy suppliers, the public has very little control over which supplier they use. Collectively, they deliver over 15 billion litres of clean water and remove and treat sewage from over 28 million properties every day! These operations use electricity and involve chemicals, all of which contribute to emissions. Ongoing capital investment in new infrastructure also has a carbon footprint. The sector is working hard to become net zero, although individual companies are responsible for their plan on how they will do this.[16]

The impact of climate change is putting pressure on water resources and the infrastructure supplying clean water and removing waste. Flooding can contaminate drinking water, and droughts affect the supply of water. The total water supply is predicted to decrease by 7% by 2045 because of climate change and limits to sustainable abstraction, leading to increased water restrictions.[16] Water UK, the trade body of the UK's water industry, runs several campaigns, including 'Water's worth saving'. Responsibility also lies with the water companies, which are being challenged to improve infrastructure and stop leakages.

The clean water from processing sewage is released back into rivers, lakes, aquifers and the sea. However, pollution from wastewater is a huge issue, with daily reports of water companies failing to meet the required standards of the quality of the water being released into our bodies of water. Water companies have invested £25 billion since 1995, and although there have been great improvements in the quality of some UK rivers, there is still the need for improvement.[17] There is a call for a national plan for rivers that involves protection by law, local empowerment and accountability. This would involve a wide range of organisations and roles, including legislators, local government, charities and environmentalists.

Apart from clean water, there are many other useful products from the processing of wastewater. Methane gas can be extracted during processing and the treated sludge can be used to make soil improvers and as a material for incineration to make heat and generate electricity. However, some of these uses do contribute to carbon emissions; therefore, other applications are being developed, such as using sludge as a filler in bricks for the construction industry.[17]

Interesting fact

A small group of people can make a huge difference. Most of us have heard about Surfers Against Sewage. This was started in Cornwall over 30 years ago by a group of people fed up with surfing in water contaminated with human waste. They now lead campaigns, provide educational material and provide many ways for individuals and communities to get involved: www.sas.org.uk.

Jobs in the water industry

A recent report on the water industry workforce highlighted that a shortage of talent is one of the main concerns as older workers retire. Another factor is the limited numbers of younger people joining the industry; however, many jobs and training opportunities are available for apprentices and graduates.[7]

To find out more about training within the water industry, visit: www.meritskills.co.uk/news/the-water-industry-skills-gap.

For an example of a website focusing on jobs in the water industry, visit: www.waterjobsuk.com. Use the search facility to see the variety of jobs in different disciplines such as science, construction and engineering.

The Energy and Utility Skills Partnership has information about industry priorities for developing a skilled, sustainable workforce for the energy and utilities sectors: www.euskills.co.uk/about/energy-utilities-skills-partnership/.

Things to think about

Encourage students to research which water company serves their schools and homes. What are the company's priorities? What are they doing to work more sustainably? What are the training and employment opportunities with the company?

Waste management

The UK waste collection, treatment and disposal sector employs about 123,400 people.[18] Waste management is a complicated sector and involves:

- household;
- industrial;
- medical;
- nuclear;
- construction and demolition waste.

UK households produce over 26 million tonnes each year and just under half is recycled (nearly 57% in Scotland). A large proportion goes to landfill, and a small amount is incinerated to generate heat energy and electricity.

First, the waste is sent to a processing facility and is sorted into organic and inorganic materials. The organic material, such as food and garden waste, can be composted to make fertiliser and soil improvers. Inorganic material is separated into recyclable and non-recyclable, with the latter sent to landfill. Developments in landfill technology ensure contamination into the soils and groundwater is prevented. The recyclable materials (paper, plastics and metals) are sent to specialist facilities for processing. 'Simpler Recycling' legislation came into effect in England in March 2025, requiring every business to have at least three bin types: general waste, dry-mixed recycling and food waste.[19,20]

Recycling, especially plastics, is a complicated business. As technology has developed, processing facilities can sort different types of plastic using optical sorters, shred and prepare them to form plastic pellets that can be used to make new products. Although the waste management sector has yet to push career pathways with young people, there is lots of evidence-based information to engage students about recycling. For examples visit:

- www.plasticrecyclingfacts.org
- www.recyclenow.com

Things to think about

Blister packs, used to safely package tablets, contain a mixture of metal foil and plastic and so are difficult to recycle. Some companies offer a collection and recycling service, but it is costly. Perhaps the young people you support could come up with a solution to encourage their local community to recycle their medication blister packs. For ideas visit: www.recyclenow.com/how-to-recycle/recycling-medicine-packaging.

The circular economy

More recycling isn't enough. You may have heard of the term circular economy, based on three principles:[21]

- Eliminate waste and pollution.
- Circulate products and materials.
- Regenerate nature.

The idea is to keep materials in circulation by refurbishing, maintaining or reprocessing, rather than just recycling. For this to work, regulation that reduces consumption is required, and designers and manufacturers are needed who understand the principles of the circular economy. This will require 'circular skills', the knowledge and understanding to encourage and contribute to a circular economy, such as:[22]

- Upskilling designers to understand how the materials they use in a product can be recycled, for example, man-made and natural fibres in textiles are very difficult to separate and recycle at the end of the garment's usefulness.
- Enable manufacturers to understand the economics of recycling their products and how this can be made financially viable.
- Support waste management professionals to be able to feed back on recycling problems to manufacturers, including the public sector.
- Educate policymakers so that regulations are streamlined to encourage a circular economy and penalise excessive waste production.

One important component of the circular economy is to regenerate nature. The idea is that 'waste' is a human concept and in nature, nothing is wasted, just regenerated, such as leaves falling from trees and returning material to the soil. In a circular economy, regenerative farming practices are encouraged that actively improve nature, organic waste from society is composted and used for soil regeneration, and urban areas include dense planting that provides habitats, absorbs rainwater and filters the air. For more information about the role agriculture has to play in the move to net zero and nature restoration, see chapter 6.

> **World of work example: The Environmental Services Association (ESA)**
>
> ESA is a trade association for recycling and waste treatment service providers, supporting the move towards a circular economy across the UK. You'll find up-to-date information and research in their news section on the website: https://esauk.org/news/.
>
> **How this is useful:**
>
> Begin by sharing the waste flow diagram with students. What activities do they recognise, or learn about, at school? Are there facilities nearby, for example, reprocessing energy from waste (https://esauk.org/recycling-and-waste-management-in-the-uk/how-does-the-sector-work/)?

Jobs in the waste management industry

Careers in this sector involve studying subjects such as chemical engineering, materials science and mechanical engineering. Operational roles are vital too, such as mechanics, plant operatives and injection moulding technicians.

The Chartered Institution of Wastes Management (CIWM) is 'the leading professional membership organisation for individuals in the sustainability, resources and waste management sector'. Their jobs website is a great resource for young people to learn about current job opportunities and the skills, qualifications and experience required: https://ciwmjobs.co.uk/.

The jobs board for waste and recycling experts is also a useful resource: www.wastejobsuk.com.

To find out more about the range of different types of jobs that will be required in the circular economy, visit: www.circle-economy.com/circular-jobs-initiative/circular-jobs.

Sustainable Careers

 World of work example: NI Water

NI Water provides water and sewage services in Northern Ireland. Their Climate Change strategy is a commercial example of how energy, water and waste management and conservation are all linked together.

How this is useful:

Encourage young people to explore the website to find out how the company is involved in peatland restoration and tree planting, as well as providing high-quality drinking water and investing in renewable energy production: www.niwater.com/climatechange/.

More information about: Transport and the global supply chain

The logistics sector can be overlooked by careers professionals and teachers, but young people need to think about the road, rail, air and sea industries and how technological developments may affect them and provide future career opportunities. A good place to start is: https://logistics.org.uk/about-us.

Transport and the global supply chain are some of the biggest greenhouse gas emitters in the world. While there is much that the individual can control about their travel choices, the biggest impact will be from research and development for new fuels and technologies (in shipping, aviation, rail and automotive) that are carbon zero: www.theecoexperts.co.uk/news/top-7-most-polluting-industries.

For more information about environmental campaigns, news, research and policy updates in the UK logistics sector, visit: https://logistics.org.uk/environment.

Unipart is embracing the race to help logistics and the supply chain become net zero. They have cut transport emissions through the use of biofuels in their vehicles, are working on a pilot to support the NHS with electric vehicles and are adapting their expertise to the circular economy of electric vehicle batteries. Visit their website for more information: www.unipart.com.

For information about careers in the logistics sector visit: https://generationlogistics.org/.

> **Interesting fact**
>
> By 2040, all HGV trucks in the UK will need to have zero emissions. HVS was launched in 2017 to innovate hydrogen-electric, carbon-free HGV technology. Encourage young people to explore their website to find out about the skills and experiences of their team, the company values and current job opportunities: www.hvs.co.uk.

Conservation

To regenerate nature is one of the three principles of the circular economy, and conservation is the sector that will help us to do this. Once on the periphery of industry and the economy, the conservation sector is now understood to be a key player in the transition to net zero and nature recovery. This section will focus on three themes; biodiversity, natural carbon capture and water management. A mini case study of the Woodland Trust's Glen Finglas Estate is included to illustrate how these themes are interlinked and beneficial for more than just a local site.

Biodiversity

Biodiversity is the variety of plants, animals, fungi and microorganisms. The more biodiverse an area is, the more likely it will be able to cope with environmental pressures such as drought and flooding. Human activities are affecting the balance of nature in many ways. Climate change is high on the public agenda, but our direct effect on biodiversity is often overlooked. Intensive farming practices can harm habitats where important insects live; in turn, this is affecting the pollination rates of plants, including food crops.[23] Agricultural techniques are also affecting soil quality, causing a vicious cycle of relying on artificial fertilisers. The lack of predators in the UK has caused the numbers of herbivores, such as deer and rabbits, to rise, which affects natural habitats, crops and woodland plantations. The environment, economy and society are interlinked, and the negative effects on our 'natural capital', such as pollution, the threat of flooding and lack of access to recreation places, are affecting the economy and society's health and well-being.[23]

Understanding the population of species in the UK is vital, and the National Biodiversity Network (NBN) is a data-sharing partnership between charities, government agencies and businesses. The data is used by policymakers, conservationists and development companies carrying out impact assessments. To help schools allow students to connect in a meaningful way with nature, NBN has also led the development of a free programme for schools called the National Education Nature Park (see the resources section in chapter 9 for more information).

The importance of improving our biodiversity is recognised in legislation, with the biodiversity net gain (BNG) now mandatory in all building developments in England. The development must give a 10% increase in the biodiversity value compared to the pre-development habitat. However, this can be achieved off-site (e.g. by buying biodiversity units from a specialist organisation) or by financing the government to invest in biodiversity via 'statutory biodiversity credits'.[24]

Natural carbon capture

Nature-based solutions are being used to actively reduce the amount of carbon dioxide in the atmosphere. There are two main ways this is done: plants absorb carbon dioxide during photosynthesis, and peat-rich soils act as a long-term store of carbon in the organic matter in the ground. There are many projects involving the protection and development of habitats such as woodland, meadows and grasslands increasing plant populations and therefore the rate of photosynthesis. There is also work being done by charities and landowners to restore peatland across the UK, and their work can be validated by the Peatland Code.[25]

Peatland restoration and the creation of new woodland are off track, and according to the Climate Change Committee, both need to double to meet the UK's targets of creating 30,000 hectares of new woodland per year by 2025 and restoring 32,000 hectares of peatland per year by 2026.[26] Read the mini case study to find out about what the Woodland Trust is doing to restore upland expanses of peat.

Water

Conservation methods are used to slow down water movement over land and reduce flooding in rivers in lowlands and towns. Natural flood management restores, or mimics, the way nature slows down the movement of water in rivers or floodplains. This can be upstream in uplands, where water is held back by tree planting and the removal of moorland drainage, reducing the risk of flooding in lowlands. It can also involve reshaping rivers through farmland to remove the straightened pathway installed during past centuries.[27]

There is a wide range of projects across England supported by the government and partner agencies such as the National Trust, local wildlife trusts, rivers trusts, farmers and other landowners. Visit the government's website to find out if there is a project near you.[28]

MINI CASE STUDY – WOODLAND TRUST, GLEN FINGLAS ESTATE

The Woodland Trust is the largest woodland conservation charity in the UK. In 1996, they took ownership of their largest site, a former hill farm in the heart of the Trossachs in central Scotland forming the Glen Finglas Estate. For over 25 years, they have protected ancient woodland, created new native woods and developed a mosaic of habitats including grassland, marshland and moorland.

From high mountain tops to the shores of lochs, the Woodland Trust manages a site that contributes to the local economy via jobs and tourism, generates renewable energy through two hydro schemes and mitigates against climate change via carbon capture and flood prevention in their restored peatland and tree planting schemes. Farming has continued on the estate, although the practices are much different with stock numbers of sheep reduced and a special, hardy breed of cattle, Luing, introduced that helps to maintain the upland pastures as they would have been pre-industrialisation.

Owning this land for over two decades has enabled the Woodland Trust to gather vast amounts of data that are used to inform the monitoring of endangered species, such as wildcats and montane scrub, and in the research of regenerative upland farming methods, including how grazing impacts grassland biodiversity.

The Woodland Trust wants the public to benefit from their work in Glen Finglas. Recreation and well-being are high on the agenda with new footpaths, information displays and seasonal events to educate and provide a space for relaxation and connecting with nature. Volunteering is key to how the Woodland Trust works. From educating the public to running events, surveying wildlife and taking part in habitat restoration, there are plenty of opportunities for local people to get involved.

For more information visit: www.woodlandtrust.org.uk/about-us/where-we-work/scotland/glen-finglas-25-year-transformation/.

Careers in conservation

According to Lanta, there are over 60,000 people employed in conservation in the UK. There are a range of roles and pathways from the operational level, such as field surveyor, to supervisory and senior roles involved in specialist consultancy and management.[29] Although many organisations may employ a small number of people in a conservation role, many employers are finding recruitment challenging as there are a low number of applicants with the desired skills and qualifications. The increased use of information in managing conservation has led to a rise in the demand for data scientists, software developers and financial experts with an understanding of environmental legislation.

For more information about careers in environmental conservation, visit: www.lantra.co.uk/careers/Industry/Environmental%20Conservation.

Use the filter option at www.environmentjob.co.uk/jobs for more granular job opportunities that can form the basis of discussions with young people about the qualifications, skills and experience desired by employers.

The Swift Street series of five detailed lessons explores the jobs involved, from ecology to media, in transforming the fictional, industrial Swift Street into a public green space: https://cieem.net/resource/green-jobs-for-nature-swift-street/.

For more information, videos and job profiles, including how to get a job that benefits nature, from ecology to law and media, visit:

- https://greenjobsfornature.org/
- www.conservation-careers.com/

Things to think about

The Race Report is an organisation that focuses on highlighting the need for greater diversity and inclusion in the environment sector, especially in charities linked to sustainability and climate action. They collect employee data from individual charities and share this in 'transparency cards'. As well as diversity and inclusion information from charities, there are also news, updates and blogs that your students may find useful: www.race-report.uk.

World of work example: The Institute of Sustainability and Environmental Professionals (ISEP)

Formerly the Institute of Environmental Management and Assessment (IEMA), ISEP is the professional body for those working in the environment and sustainability sector. They oversee many training courses (see chapter 7 for more information) and the chartership of environmentalists: www.iema.net.

How this is useful:

ISEP is raising awareness of green skills, and its Green Careers website contains information you can use with young people: www.greencareershub.com.

> **More information about: Green Jobs**
>
> In 2021, the Green Jobs Taskforce produced its report to the government, industry and the skills sector highlighting the types of jobs, skills and qualification levels required by a range of sectors for the UK to transition to a net zero economy. This is a useful document for teachers and career professionals as it gives you data regarding workforce projections and a list of occupations linked to all the major industries that will contribute to net zero, both directly, such as specific renewable energies, and indirectly, for example, agriculture and conservation.
>
> - www.gov.uk/government/publications/green-jsobs-taskforce-report
> - www.ons.gov.uk/economy/environmentalaccounts/bulletins/experimentalestimatesofgreenjobsuk/2024
>
> See chapter 4 for information about classifying green jobs.

Conclusion

The focus of this chapter is to explore sectors that are driving the UK to net zero and nature restoration. The energy sector may appear to be the primary player in this, as they develop renewable energy technologies, decarbonise electricity production and stabilise the UK's energy supply. But this is a complicated area, and the development of clean transport for roads, rail, sea and air also has a part to play, requiring significant investment in infrastructure and employees, as well as design and technology.

Water and waste management are often overlooked, but these sectors are vital for the safe functioning of our economy and society. We can no longer consider resources as infinite, and the concept of the circular economy is one that our young people will need to embrace during their working lives.

The profile of conservation, previously considered a niche career, has been raised as both government and industry realise that nature restoration to improve biodiversity, manage water flow and store carbon has benefits for the economy and society. New companies are emerging that offer environmental services, and the demand for ecologists, environmental lawyers and financiers with an understanding of 'green issues' is increasing.

It will take more than the three sectors discussed in this chapter to get us to net zero, and chapter 6 will explore how a variety of other sectors are striving to work more sustainably while still having a primary purpose of delivering a product or service.

To keep up to date with cutting-edge research and technological developments within the sectors and industries that are helping the UK to reach a zero-carbon economy visit: www.great.gov.uk/international/content/investment/sectors/.

Chapter 6
Sectors working in a sustainable way

> Many sectors, industries, organisations and individuals are doing what they've always done, only in a better way to minimise impact and improve society.

Introduction

Chapter 5 focused on the main sectors driving the UK towards net zero and nature restoration, namely energy, water and waste management and conservation.

This chapter is designed to give you an overview of how other sectors in the UK are responding to the net zero challenge, nature restoration and using new solutions for the benefit of local and global communities. The primary purpose for these sectors is to deliver a product or service; however, if the UK economy is to reach net zero by 2050, ALL sectors will have to be involved in decarbonisation and reducing waste. The sectors covered are mineral products, agriculture and food, construction, manufacturing, health and the creative industries. Brief outlines of the developments in green financing, hospitality and tourism and retail are also included.

Changes occur rapidly as new technologies become available and companies update their strategies, so the sector information might be out of date by the time the book is printed. Therefore, sector and industry web links will be included to signpost you to up-to-date information so that you can have relevant discussions with young people about sector developments, jobs and skills.

A note about categorising – humans naturally group similar things. So, in this book, an industry is made up of companies that do similar things and a sector comprises a group of industries whose output is all related. Here are two examples:

- The manufacturing sector includes the automotive and aerospace industries.
- The energy sector includes the generation and distribution industries.

Within each of these industries, you can search for specific businesses and find out who the local employers are and the types of job opportunities available. It can be helpful for young people to think about employers and companies in this way. A career they are interested in may give them employment in different industries or sectors; for example, someone graduating with a master's degree in pharmacy could work in the health sector as a community pharmacist or in the pharmaceutical industry as a research scientist. An electrical engineer could be involved in design, manufacturing or operations and maintenance in many sectors.

When teachers and career professionals understand how sectors are responding to the climate crisis, we can help young people consider how this might affect their lives, from the products they consume to the services they use. By exploring sectors and industries, young people can think about how these link to their values, interests and hobbies and how this may be relevant to career planning.

Sectors

Many companies are incorporating environmental and social responsibilities into their governance, and this can be seen in their strategy and key performance indicators (KPIs). This isn't just within their own business, as conditions and targets are also often set for procurement (their supply chain) and by their customers. These can involve environmental objectives such as reducing carbon emissions, water consumption and waste and increasing the positive effects on nature. Objectives can also be social, such as increasing diversity and inclusion in the workforce, improving employee well-being and working more closely with their local community.

Starting with extracting raw materials out of the ground to manufacturing and providing services, this section includes a range of sectors and how they are contributing to sustainable development. For more information about green jobs, see chapter 4; for further reading about different sectors and examples of careers, see *STEM Careers* (2nd edition).

Mineral products

The mineral products sector includes the extraction (mining and quarrying) and processing of minerals for use in construction, agriculture, pharmaceuticals and many other sectors. The sector is working hard to reduce the negative impacts of extraction, restore, and even improving biodiversity in the locations where they operate, while also collaborating with local communities that may be impacted by their operations.

Companies are working hard to encourage a diverse workforce, from engineering and environmental science to finance, sales and data analyst roles, as vacancy numbers are increasing. There have been successes, as the number of women employed in the sector is rising, but there is a skills shortage.[1] Engineering and technical skills are in the greatest demand, with new technologies driving change, such as working with automation and robotics and hydrogen vehicles. There are many opportunities for young people to become apprentices, and professional development when in employment can also include leadership training. The 2023 survey for the mineral industry also highlighted the need for employers to collaborate more with education.[1] **This report gives leverage for teachers and career professionals to contact local companies involved in quarrying, mining or mineral processing and begin discussions about how they can collaborate** (see chapter 9 for guidance).

The Minerals Matter website (https://minerals-matter.co.uk/shape-your-world/) has some great resources including developments in the sector, video links, careers information and job profiles.

 Interesting fact

Lithium is an important ingredient in batteries and the development of electrical vehicles. The race is on to source a reliable supply of lithium in the UK. Cornish Lithium is an innovative UK company focusing on sustainable approaches to mineral extraction: https://cornishlithium.com/.

Agriculture and food

This section will cover farming and food production. For selling food, see the retail section.

Farming can be high on the agenda for some people, with emotive topics such as animal welfare, soil degradation, polluting water courses, food poverty, supermarket contracts or government policy driving their concern. Yet for others, the production of the plants and animals they consume is too far removed from their day-to-day lives to be of any importance.

Everyone eats food, so this topic can be a good way to engage young people to consider sustainability and careers. Sustain, the food and farming organisation, highlights that '35% of the UK's greenhouse gas emissions come from food and drink'.[2] Therefore, for the sector to reach net zero by 2050, changes to the way crops are grown and meat produced are required. Research and development – and innovative farming practices – will lead the way, such as decarbonising the production of fertiliser. Climate change will affect food production, so research into disease-resistant crops and plants that can grow productively in wetter and milder conditions is also important.

Closely linked to food production is our health, and the National Food Strategy's independent review highlights how the nation's diet will need to change to meet net zero and address the health implications of cheap ultra-processed food high in additives.[3] The review highlights growth areas that will require new skills, such as alternative ways to produce protein (i.e. plant, insect, fermentation and cell-cultured meat). To fill the skills shortage, a qualified workforce is required and the UK will have to import these new foods if we fail to plan for this.[3]

For sustainable development education, the school canteen is a good place to start. Where does the food come from? Does the school support local suppliers? How is waste reduced and healthy eating encouraged? Read how Bedford Academy addresses this in the case study in chapter 9.

The Tasty Careers website has dedicated sections for parents, teachers and students: https://tastycareers.org.uk/.

 Interesting fact

Farm animals, such as cows, require a rich source of protein, often achieved by adding imported soya to their diet. Based in Scotland, Beta Bugs focuses on developing the genetics of black soldier flies, to provide UK farmers with a sustainable supply of protein for animal feed: www.betabugs.uk/.

> **More information about: Green financing**
>
> The UK government's Green Financing Programme has raised over £43 billion to 'finance green expenditures to help tackle climate change, biodiversity loss and other environmental challenges while creating green jobs across the UK'. [4] The six categories for this expenditure are:
>
> - Clean transportation;
> - Renewable energy;
> - Energy efficiency;
> - Pollution prevention and control;
> - Living and natural resources;
> - Climate change adaptation.[4]
>
> Of course, many companies are involved with financing sustainability projects directly. The Soil Association Exchange has been formed from a collaboration between Lloyds Bank and the Soil Association, to help farmers work more sustainably while still being profitable. For more information, visit: www.soilassociationexchange.com.

Construction

This is a huge sector and includes something for everyone:

- the creativity of good architectural design;
- using the latest digital technologies for modelling construction sites;
- working with local communities to build quality infrastructure that enhances day-to-day living;
- upgrading transport links; and
- collaborating with conservationists to ensure the negative effects of construction are minimised.

The construction sector is embracing many changes. **Diversity in the workforce is important, and many companies will actively seek engagement with schools to work with students from under-represented groups. This is great, as long as you collaborate to carefully plan the next steps following an activity (see chapter 9 for more guidance).** Many construction businesses were embracing their social and environmental responsibilities long before the UN Sustainable Development Goals (SDGs) became part of an organisation's strategic planning (see the case study about Balfour Beatty at the end of this chapter). Reaching net zero has increased the push for sustainability, with many building projects aspiring to achieve BREEAM certification, demonstrating the sustainability credentials of a building (https://breeam.com/about/).

There are many developments in the construction industry contributing towards sustainable economic, environmental and social improvements. The UK Green Building Council (UK GBC) is a network of construction companies and local authorities that are leading the sector and informing policy, offering solutions in the move towards net zero. They focus on ways to make communities more resilient to climate change and encourage nature restoration and the regeneration of buildings.[5] One example is 'domestic retrofit'. A total of 19 million homes in the UK have poor energy performance, contributing 40% of the UK's climate emissions from the built environment.[5] The UK GBC is working with academics to inform government policymakers on ways to retrofit homes to make them more energy efficient and provide financial incentives to homeowners.

The construction sector funds the Supply Chain Sustainability School. This focuses on upskilling the workforce about sustainability in construction and understanding more about the social, economic and environmental factors: www.supplychainschool.co.uk/about/.

For more information about a range of careers in construction and sector developments, visit the Go Construct website: www.goconstruct.org.

Interesting fact

A new build is not always the answer. Many organisations are redeveloping existing buildings, repurposing materials to reduce landfill and improving the social spaces they occupy. The Entopia project is one such example; this former 1930s telephone exchange in Cambridge now houses small businesses involved in sustainability innovation and uses 15% of the energy that the original building did: www.cisl.cam.ac.uk/building-entopia.

World of work example: Arup

Arup is a global company that employs designers, engineers and technical experts. They are driven by their six values:

1. Quality of work;
2. Total architecture;
3. Humane organisation;
4. Straight and honourable dealings;
5. Social usefulness;
6. Reasonable prosperity of members.

Chapter 6: Sectors Working in a Sustainable Way

How this is useful:

Encourage students to explore Arup's website. What UK projects have Arup been involved with? Are they located nearby? What jobs have been created? Could a visit be arranged?

Facilitate a discussion about Arup's six values. How do young people feel about these? Is profit or social value more important, or are they both equal and why (www.arup.com/)?

More information about: Scope emissions

When you are reading company reports or a sustainability strategy, you may come across the terms Scope 1, Scope 2 and Scope 3 emissions. This is related to the business's direct and indirect greenhouse gas emissions.

- Scope 1 emissions: From the organisation directly, such as fuel used in its buildings and vehicles.
- Scope 2 emissions: From the energy purchased from suppliers, such as electricity and heat.
- Scope 3 emissions: From the supply chain and when consumers use the product or service.

Scope 1 emissions are the easiest for a company to control and therefore reduce. A company can choose to use renewable energy, so Scope 2 is relatively easy for a company to control and reduce, too. Scope 3 often contributes most to a company's carbon footprint. It is complex and therefore difficult to control, requiring suppliers to provide data about the carbon footprint of their product or services.

Organisations trying to become net zero will need to obtain and use data about the carbon footprint of their building and vehicles, energy supply and the services and materials they use. Employees in a variety of departments, such as procurement, marketing, sales and manufacturing, will need to know how to evaluate the data, decide how reliable it is and use the information to help reduce their company's greenhouse emissions.

Many business-to-business companies exist that offer services to calculate carbon footprints.

For more information visit: www.mckinsey.com/featured-insights/mckinsey-explainers/what-are-scope-1-2-and-3-emissions.

>  **Things to think about**
>
> What are the Scope 1, 2 and 3 emissions strategies for your local authority/school/college? How could you share this information with students? How could you encourage students to get involved with the school/college in reducing its Scope 1, 2 and 3 emissions?

Manufacturing

From vehicles to white goods, pharmaceuticals to food, the UK manufacturing sector covers a broad range of industries and provides 2.6 million jobs, with the northwest of England leading the UK's manufacturing.[6] There isn't the space in this book to explore each manufacturing industry, but the principles of working sustainably are transferrable across all sectors and there are many ways that manufacturers are improving their operating standards:

- Reducing consumption of energy and water;
- Increasing use of automation and artificial intelligence (AI);
- Minimising the production of waste;
- Improving the life cycle of the products;
- Interrogating the supply chain.

Many companies are investing in product development and sustainable practices, with research and development high on the agenda. Make UK has launched *Electrify Industry* to help the sector overcome the hurdles of using electricity while also decarbonising its business.[6] Developments in the use of robotics and AI have the potential to increase productivity; however, a lack of knowledge about how to adopt new technologies and a workforce with the operational skills to use them is affecting productivity.[7]

Upskilling existing employees' digital and technological skills, recruiting new staff with the desired skills and retaining those employees with the talents required are now the focus of many businesses in the manufacturing sector. The 2024 report from Barclays shows that manufacturing leaders are concerned that young people do not envisage a career in the sector. However, 53% of manufacturers are not engaging with young people in secondary education.[8] **Perhaps this is the time for schools to approach their local manufacturers, to discuss how they can work in partnership to inform young people about careers in manufacturing and help secure future talent.**

Chapter 6: Sectors Working in a Sustainable Way

Environmental, social and governance (ESG) targets are gaining prominence among manufacturing businesses, with 74% having ESG conditions in their procurement (supply chain) policies. These conditions may include health and safety, human and labour rights, for example, within supplier companies. Waste management, reducing packaging, recycling and efficient use of water are also important ESG conditions for many manufacturing businesses, with larger companies generally further ahead with their strategies than smaller companies (see chapter 7 for more information about related qualifications, such as Level 3 Energy Efficiency and Sustainability). [9]

For more information about developments and issues in manufacturing, visit the sector's website Make UK: www.makeuk.org/.

Things to think about

Manufacturing is an important sector in the UK. Sometimes a product may be designed in the UK, but where is it manufactured? Which of the products that you use are manufactured in the UK? How can we help young people to learn more about possible careers in UK manufacturing? Encourage students to explore the websites of local manufacturing companies. How are they working more sustainably? What are the job and training opportunities? How can you help your students to gain the skills required (see chapter 9 for more information about working with employers, for example, planning skills bootcamps)?

More information about: Hospitality and tourism

UK Hospitality is the trade body for hospitality in the UK. Its website has data about hospitality's contribution to employment in your area: www.ukhospitality.org.uk.

The sector is also working hard to help companies reach their sustainability targets, through a partnership with the Zero Carbon Forum and their carbon footprint calculator: https://zerocarbonforum.com/.

For those organisations ready to gain recognition, the Green Tourism certificates in bronze, silver and gold are available: www.green-tourism.com.

Health

Across the world, climate change is affecting people's health, for example, heat-related deaths and poor health due to air and water pollution.[10] The healthcare sector is directly linked to Sustainable Development Goal 3 (good health and well-being); however, the sector has negative impacts on the environment due to energy usage and pollutants released.

In 2017, the World Health Organization offered a strategic document to help countries develop environmentally sustainable health systems. Their 10 recommendations fit into three broad categories: targeted policies and improved management, sustainable procurement and reducing waste and using the healthcare workforce and communities they serve as agents of change.[11]

The NHS is the UK's largest employer and is responsible for about 4% of the country's carbon emissions. The Health and Care Act (2022) sets out the pathway to net zero by 2045. This includes reducing energy consumption in buildings and transport and reducing water consumption and waste production. Innovations in medicine production and business infrastructure are also contributing to more sustainable practices. Change will involve many people, employees and patients, all playing their part to make a difference. For example, procurement staff will need to question the supply chain: how are the goods manufactured? Are items single-use and if so how can they be recycled?[12] **The NHS is keen to promote careers within the organisation. Perhaps liaise with your local NHS organisation to find out how they can inform your students about NHS careers and how they work sustainably**. For more information, visit: www.healthcareers.nhs.uk/career-planning/career-planning/career-advisers-and-teachers.

The health sector in the UK also involves many other organisations, such as social care providers, dentists, opticians and private providers of healthcare such as BUPA. Increasingly, sustainability is becoming part of their strategy and day-to-day practice, from offering recycling services for their products to using electric vehicles within their fleet.

 Interesting fact

The propellant in some asthma inhalers, such as Ventolin, has a greenhouse effect, and 3% of the NHS's carbon emissions are from inhalers. Inhalers are vital, but it is important for patients to use and dispose of them correctly. Patients with asthma may be offered alternative inhalers with less, or no, propellant, such as dry powder inhalers.[13]

More information about: Retail

In 2022, retail employed 2.7 million people, and data from 2023 shows the sector contributed 4.7% to the UK's total economic output.[14] However, retail is facing pressures from the cost of living crisis and changing consumer behaviour, such as buying online. Business consultant Crowe reports that sustainability is a complex area both for retailers and consumers. However, they identify that it is 'strategically imperative' for retailers to interrogate their own environmental, social and governance (ESG) credentials, as consumers become more aware and make informed choices: www.crowe.com/uk/insights/retailers-role-on-sustainability.

Transform Our World has developed a resource to help you discuss consumerism and excessive consumption with your students, including the impact of advertising and the origin of everyday products: www.transform-our-world.org/good-life-schools#black-friday.

Creative industries sector

In 2023, the creative industries sector employed 2.4 million people, and in 2022 the sector contributed 5.7% to the UK's total economic output.[14] The sector is working hard to reduce its carbon footprint and promote more sustainable ways of working. In 2022, the Creative Industries Policy and Evidence Centre commissioned a report into the creative industries' response to the climate emergency and its path to net zero. The range of industries within this sector is vast, from architecture, to film and television, to gaming, music and fashion. The report looks at each industry, examining the environmental impact, path to sustainability, obstacles to progress and priorities for further research.

Read the report here: www.culturehive.co.uk/resources/creative-industries-and-the-climate-emergency-the-path-to-net-zero/.

The gaming industry continues to grow in the UK as people of all ages take part in a variety of activities on their phones, consoles and computers. There is a huge range of roles, for example, hardware and software developers, musicians, marketing and tech finance experts. Each stage of the gaming industry impacts the environment and as the popularity increases, the gaming industry is beginning to address some of the challenges. Tech investor UNlty Ventures has investigated how the gaming industry can be more sustainable:[15]

- Reducing waste – Many companies are reducing the packaging of new systems and encouraging users to keep their hardware for a long time and recycle items when they need upgrading.

- Reducing energy consumption and carbon emissions – Gaming consoles use twice the energy that laptops do, therefore designers are challenged to create more energy-efficient equipment.
- Mining for raw materials – Working with suppliers that mine responsibly for metals, such as copper and nickel, used in the electronic components of hardware.
- Renewable energy – Use of renewable energy sources to power servers used in cloud gaming and the cooling systems used to control the temperature of servers and data centres.

The creative industries are keen to raise the profile of careers within the sector. The charity Into Film has a wealth of resources about how the industry is working more sustainably. Just search for 'sustainability' on their website for up-to-date resources: www.intofilm.org.

For developments in UK creative industries, visit: www.thecreativeindustries.co.uk/about-us.

For specific information about careers, visit: https://discovercreative.careers/.

 Interesting fact

DF Concerts & Events is a Scottish business striving to make live music more sustainable. They invest in sustainably sourced biofuels, improve recycling by recovering materials and have introduced carbon literacy training for staff: www.dfconcertsandevents.com/.

 Interesting fact

Cotton is an important raw material in the fashion industry and is the most commonly used fibre on the planet. However, growing cotton uses a lot of water and chemicals such as pesticides. The Soil Association is working hard to improve the production of cotton, relying on natural, sustainable systems. There is a very accessible video on their website that you could share with students: www.soilassociation.org/take-action/organic-living/fashion-textiles/organic-cotton/.

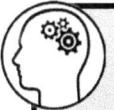

Things to think about

TV and film can change lives (think about the impact of the TV series *Mr Bates vs The Post Office*)! Founded in 2011, the organisation Albert helps the TV and film industries to reduce the environmental impact of their productions and encourages content creators to raise the profile of environmental awareness and climate change in the work they produce. Encourage young people to be critical of some of the productions they watch. Are environmental messages included? How do they feel about this? Do the programmes they watch have the 'Albert footprint' on the end credits? What does this mean (https://wearealbert.org/)?

World of work example: UN Global Compact Network UK

This is a not-for-profit organisation that promotes charitable sustainable development within UK businesses. They are linked with the United Nations global collective, working with businesses to improve human rights and the environment, supporting the UN SDGs.

How this is useful:

Explore the website to find examples of UK companies that put the UN SDGs at the heart of how they operate. If your school is considering embedding the UN SDGs into its curriculum, the annual reports are a great source of company examples that you can share with subject teachers: www.unglobalcompact.org.uk/.

Conclusion

Cutting-edge technology, pioneering innovators and government policy can drive the changes needed to make our world a better place for now and future generations. This will bring lots of job opportunities and the chance to work locally, nationally and globally. It's our job to help young people to see this can benefit their future careers.

The government is committed to the UK reaching net zero by 2050, in line with the Paris Agreement (see chapter 1 for more information). Therefore, all sectors are responding by finding ways to work more sustainably. There isn't room in this chapter to address every sector, so areas that are important to the UK economy and (hopefully) of interest to young people were selected to give insights into examples of exciting developments (for more information about sectors, see *STEM Careers*, 2nd edition).

If you are a teacher, you and your students can explore the net zero commitments and strategies of some of the companies that make equipment used in class or employ people with qualifications that your subject can lead to. Does the company align its mission and values to any of the UN SDGs? For example, history, art and performing arts teachers can encourage their students to find out how venues, museums and galleries are working more sustainably.

There are familiar themes in all sectors, such as interrogating the supply chain, reducing energy and water consumption, using energy from renewable sources, reducing carbon emissions from transport, reducing waste and packaging and considering the life cycle of the product (circular or recycling). Careers professionals can help young people to understand that just about every person working for an organisation has a part to play. This will increasingly become part of most job descriptions, and we can help young people to embrace this and develop the skills and behaviours to succeed in the role. Ongoing learning and professional development will become more important for the majority of the workforce, from care workers learning to use apps to record client information to farmers embracing the data that satellite imaging can provide. There will be the opportunity to learn new skills and how to use new technology. To help your students to feel satisfaction at work, encourage them to accept this as the norm.

The next chapter will explore learning and qualifications that are directly linked to sustainability, for teachers, careers professionals, students at school and beyond.

 **CASE STUDY 1 – BALFOUR BEATTY**

This case study will give you an example of a well-known company, Balfour Beatty, that delivers infrastructure in a range of sectors and has 'Sustainable' as one of its core values.

By learning more about a company such as Balfour Beatty, young people can understand how human-centric qualities are just as valuable to an employer as technical skills and knowledge.

About the company

Balfour Beatty is an international infrastructure group, working in the UK, United States and Hong Kong. It is the largest construction and infrastructure provider in the UK, employing 12,000 people. A multidisciplinary organisation, Balfour Beatty's business model involves their teams in infrastructure investments, construction services and support services working closely together to deliver high-quality outcomes for its customers.

Sustainability and Balfour Beatty

Joanna Gilroy was appointed Group Director of Sustainability in 2022. Jo is passionate about sustainability, highlighting, 'Sustainability should be understood as a business movement, as well as an environmental one. All businesses, regardless of where they operate or what they do, rely on natural resources, or natural capital, and people, or social capital, in order to be in business. For example, imagine what would happen to Balfour Beatty's operations if we could no longer buy steel, or if young engineers did not want to work for us. What would happen? We would cease to operate. To be sustainable, businesses need to understand that their success depends upon three equally important sources of value.'

Jo explains, 'Business has always measured value in one way, by profit, money in / money out, and you will want more money in than money out. Yet every business on the planet and not just business, every society, every economy, actually has three sources of value, which are intrinsically linked and equally as important to each other. Every society, community and business does need money. You need money to invest and develop things. But every society, economy and business also depends upon natural capital which are the natural resources that the economy or society or business simply cannot survive without. Equally they also depend upon social capital – all of the people, suppliers, customers, diverse workforces, that makes those economies, societies and businesses stronger.'

'And all sustainability says is that if our businesses, economies and societies do not understand, protect and equally invest in their three sources of value: natural; social and financial, if they allow one source of value to dominate over the other two, then they will be disrupted, and those disruptions come in the form of climate change, areas of poverty, areas of low economic mobility, water scarcity, falling crop rates, increased pests, air pollution, to name a few.'

In 2024, Balfour Beatty launched the latest evolution of its Building New Futures Sustainability Strategy which seeks to prioritise and protect the business' sources of natural and social value. Under Jo's leadership, the strategy is more holistic, with a 'think global, act local' approach to protecting and enhancing the environment and leaving a positive social legacy. This sustainability strategy is more than just words, as there are measurable targets set for each of the six focus areas:

1. Climate change;
2. Nature positive;
3. Resource efficiency;
4. Supply chain integrity;
5. Community engagement;
6. Employee diversity, equity and inclusion.

The Sustainability Community

To deliver the new strategy, the board has invested in the sustainability function, and Jo began to form a community of people, from different teams and backgrounds, who can influence the success of the strategy.

She knew that this community couldn't just include environmentalists and social impact specialists. It needed to be reflective of the business, including procurement specialists with a sustainable mindset; comms people, who can market and articulate the company's sustainability priorities; engineers and operational people who can design bridges, public buildings and roads to be as sustainable as possible. The community includes material engineers, IT and data engineers and energy specialists who all learn and develop a sustainability mindset and then take this out to support the different business units in Balfour Beatty, driving sustainability forward, sharing, educating and supporting those wider teams to be better.

Sustainable working across Balfour Beatty

The profile of sustainability is kept at the forefront of how Balfour Beatty operates as each business unit has sustainability professionals, working strategically and operationally, and a sustainability director who is responsible for developing action plans aligned to the Group's sustainability focus areas and targets.

Each project, for example, building or upgrading a road, has the support of the sustainability specialists required for that particular project. These could be carbon specialists, environmental compliance specialists, energy managers, ecology specialists or involved in social impact, such as working with local schools and communities. This supports the 'act local' that is essential for the strategy delivery.

Jo says, 'It is just about making sure that we've got these individuals around these decision-making tables.' She goes on to describe one example at a road building project: 'we've got a single director that is responsible, so that falls within their remit and then we've got biodiversity and ecology specialists who support the project with wildlife restoration because we're building a green bridge there and it's got to be the right green bridge. You can't just plant any tree or bit of foliage.'

Jo reflects, 'This is the largest sustainability group I've ever had the privilege of working with and it is reflective of the change Balfour Beatty has gone through, but also the expectations in our industry. Construction is one of the largest polluters across everything, whether you're talking about air pollution, water pollution or carbon. (www.theecoexperts.co.uk/news/top-7-most-polluting-industries) Which means that one small change that we make, that is sustainable, has significant benefit.'

The Balfour Beatty way

Balfour Beatty, a company of engineers, has a 'can do' attitude, with 'Make a Difference' being one of the core behaviours it expects from everyone who works for or with them. The sustainability function has embraced this attitude as Jo explains, 'Sustainability presents the challenge of here's a big problem. How do we solve it?' The company has five values and encourages five behaviours, including collaborating and talking positively, which Jo says support the sustainability agenda.

There is an expectation from clients that Balfour Beatty will use their scale and leverage to influence changes in the supply chain, challenging all involved, from suppliers to subcontractors, to do better. An example is when working with energy suppliers to deliver the renewable energy infrastructure that the UK needs. To achieve this, Balfour Beatty realised they needed to be ambitious and has set out a target to become net zero by 2050, contributing to the decarbonising of the sector overall.

Balfour Beatty values

- We're Lean: We create value for our customers and drive continuous improvement.
- We're Expert: Our highly skilled colleagues and partners set us apart.
- We're Trusted: We deliver on our promises and we do the right thing.
- We're Safe: We make safety personal.
- We're Sustainable: We act responsibly to protect and enhance our planet and society.

Balfour Beatty behaviours

- Talk positively.
- Collaborate relentlessly.
- Encourage constantly.

- Make a difference.
- Value everyone.

Balfour Beatty's future workforce

The construction sector is growing. There is much work that needs doing, to build climate-resilient infrastructure and ensure that existing infrastructure, such as roads and rail, is fit for the future. However, the world of business has changed. In the past, resources were plentiful and businesses could be wasteful with energy, materials and people, but those days are gone. Jo reiterates that sustainability concerns economic, environmental and social capital. And people matter to Balfour Beatty. The available workforce is not as large as it used to be and therefore the company values their current employees, provides learning and development opportunities and works hard to attract future talent.

Jo summarises the wider construction industry's concerns. 'The majority of the workers in construction are older and they're coming towards the time when they'll want to retire. Who's going to replace them?' (https://constructionmanagement.co.uk/constructions-ageing-workforce-where-are-the-next-generation/). Any business has to think about how it will find its future workforce, so how does Balfour Beatty do this? Jo suggests, 'You've got to be current and relevant to the needs and the attitudes of the emerging workforce, or the talent will go elsewhere.'

How do these more traditional companies attract a younger workforce? With sustainability as a core value, Balfour Beatty hopes they are relevant to potential employees who care about their future and want to work for a company that's part of the solution, not the problem.

As one of the six sustainability focus areas, Balfour Beatty is driven by the need for diversity, equity and inclusion in the workforce. In terms of their future workforce, diversity could not be more critical, providing strength and resilience. Jo compares this to nature: 'Every living environment on the planet teaches us that diversity is the lifeblood of strength and resilience. Diversity is absolutely everything. It's the same for a business. If you have got individuals in your business that think the same way, when you come across a problem that you haven't encountered before, which you will, everyone's going to approach it the same way.' Therefore, it is important for Balfour Beatty to engage with schoolchildren, from primary age, from a range of different backgrounds at the point that they're thinking about what they might do when they've grown up. As part of their social value commitments, there is the opportunity for local projects to work with schools and community groups.

Leo Quinn, Balfour Beatty's Group Chief Executive, has long understood the need to nurture people at the start of their careers and in 2013 founded The 5% Club. This organisation encourages businesses to pledge to have at least 5% of their workforce in an 'earn and learn' position, such as trainees, apprentices or graduates. In 2023, 7.4% of Balfour Beatty's UK workforce was on one of the 'earn and learn' schemes.

What is Balfour Beatty looking for in their future workforce?

The core values and behaviours are central to how Balfour Beatty operates. They are looking for potential employees who *talk positively, collaborate relentlessly, encourage constantly, make a difference and value everyone*. Jo advises having the 'can do' attitude is very important to Balfour Beatty. She also adds, 'We need change agents that come in and challenge everyone else to up their game and be better.'

To conclude, Jo gives an example of how Balfour Beatty enables its younger workforce to question and challenge, describing a concept that two of her teams have set up called the 'sustainability sprouts' where people at the beginning of their careers come together and engage directly with managers. 'They are the best spotlight. They are the best mirror of yourself as a leader as to whether you are actually doing a good job. I don't think young people realise the power that they have at all. Our sustainability sprouts hold me and my team to account, and we ask them, "Are we doing a good enough job?" they tell us the most invaluable of things that we can learn and adapt from.'

For more information about Balfour Beatty, visit: www.balfourbeatty.com.

To find out more about The 5% Club, visit: www.5percentclub.org.uk.

Chapter 7
Qualifications in sustainability

> Whatever stage of education and career, focus on learning the details about sustainability in order to make a difference.

Introduction

The three themes running through this book are sustainability and careers, having a sustainable career and sustainable development education (SDE). SDE involves two concepts:

1. Teaching students **about** sustainable development, for example, as done in science and geography, so that they have the subject knowledge.

2. Teaching **for** sustainable development so that young people develop the values and skills to become globally aware citizens who can contribute to a just and sustainable world.

This chapter will focus on the first idea: courses and qualifications linked to environmental sustainability. Teaching *for* sustainable development is covered in chapters 2 and 9.

How confident do you feel in discussing and teaching about sustainable development with the young people you work with? Courses to help you as a teacher or career professional understand more about sustainability will be introduced. Then, some of the current qualifications linked to sustainability available for secondary, further and higher education will be highlighted. The secondary school curriculum is jam-packed, but could your school consider investigating one of the recognised courses available for young people aged 14 and above?

Many industries have their own sustainability-linked qualifications, and some of these will be reviewed to give you an insight into the range of career development opportunities across the sectors. By sharing these examples with young people, you can show that employees can continue their professional development while working and gain sustainability qualifications linked to their sector.

The chapter will conclude with examples from the world of work and a detailed case study of the work of a sustainable development manager.

Training for teachers and career professionals

A good starting point for anyone who works in a school is the 35-minute video produced by University College London (UCL)'s Centre for Climate Change and Sustainability Education.[1] This helps teachers to see the place of sustainability across the curriculum, not just in geography and science. The video also leads the viewer to think about how the school itself can function in a more environmentally sustainable way, with contributors giving examples from their schools. Some of the schools highlighted are using the Sustainable Development Goals as a framework for embedding sustainability into the curriculum and functioning of the school. The video also includes how developing agency with climate action can help to improve children's mental health and well-being.

For more information, the UK Schools Sustainability Network has produced a one-hour video and audit template that you could use with staff: www.youtube.com/watch?v=pbbyzLhmKkk.

There is also a free teacher professional development online programme from UCL – Teaching for Sustainable Futures. At the time of writing, there are modules for primary and secondary maths, English, history and geography, with science modules available soon. It is recommended that 90 minutes are set aside for each module.

Other courses for teachers exist, some with a cost, for example, Future Learn's Introduction to Teaching Sustainability and Climate Action. Developed by the University of Glasgow, this course introduces the concept of ecopedagogy, examining how this approach can transform education for sustainable development.[2] Developed for southern African teachers, UNESCO's Sustainability Starts with Teachers is a free course designed to transform teaching practice by focusing on a 'change project'.[3] This five-step programme contains actions that may be useful to teachers in the Global North who are considering piloting a SDE project.

Perhaps carbon literacy training would be useful for you, other staff and your students. Formal training will help to improve knowledge related to the effect of greenhouse gases on climate change and biodiversity, empowering individuals and organisations to make changes for a just transition to net zero. It is worth doing your research, as several providers are operating in the UK and they do charge. The Carbon Literacy Project has training bespoke for different sectors, including a Carbon Literacy Toolkit for Education. Positive Planet has worked with many well-known companies, helping teams to work together to help their organisation work more sustainably. Not ready to commit too much time? Udemy offers a primer short course on sustainability, climate and carbon reduction.

Although not a training course, the Education and Training Foundation offers a full range of resources for SDE and by joining their mailing list you can keep up to date with their research and resources.[4]

If making changes across the school is too big a step at the moment, you could start by developing your knowledge of green skills with a course such as Green Skills Unlocked, offered by Energising Futures.[5] Although designed for science teachers, enrolling on this free course gives access to a green skills framework and toolkit for use in the classroom.

Scottish teachers and lecturers can make contact with the Learning for Sustainability Scotland organisation. They aim to support all aspects of learning about sustainable development, outdoor education, global citizenship and social welfare: https://learningforsustainabilityscotland.org/. There are professional learning opportunities, case study resources, and you can sign up to receive regular news updates.

Aligned to the Well-being of Future Generations (Wales) Act passed in 2015, the Curriculum for Wales aims to empower teachers with the creative freedom to enable their students to become 'ethical, informed global citizens'.[6] For those not familiar with the Welsh education system, Jones' blog (2021) contains useful references to SDE that are useful across the UK.[6]

If you are ready to take on more responsibility for sustainability in school or college, the Institute of Environmental Management and Assessment (IEMA) is a good place to start as they have a Sustainability Skills map built around 13 competencies linked to technical knowledge and sustainability leadership, as well as certified and accredited courses. (NB to better reflect the work of the organisation, they are changing their name to the Institute of Sustainability and Environmental Professionals (ISEP).)

Secondary school courses

Is the UK curriculum too narrow? Where is the space to learn about issues relating to sustainability such as resource management, climate change, nature restoration and energy security? The government has announced that an independent review of the English national curriculum will take place, with the recommendations due to be published in 2025. Let us hope that SDE is included.

Qualifications do already exist. In Scotland, there are the Environmental Science qualifications (National 3, 4, 5 and Higher), focusing on understanding and investigating biodiversity, sustainability and the Earth's resources and developing an awareness of political action and the influence of the economy. Environmental Science A Level is available in the rest of the UK. The Scottish Qualifications Authority (SQA) also offers Skills for Work courses that focus on employability. Their 'Energy' National 5 specifically focuses on renewable energy, and 'Food and Drink Manufacturing Industry' National 5 includes the importance of recycling and reducing waste.

The Welsh Baccalaureate is a non-compulsory programme offered at levels 1, 2 (GCSE equivalent) and 3 (A Level equivalent). The focus is to develop employability skills to achieve the Skills Challenge Certificate. The learner does this through four components, including a Global Citizenship Challenge and a Community Challenge.[7] Sustrans have created support material for teachers delivering the Global Citizenship Challenge Welsh Baccalaureate to Key Stage 4 students.[8]

The Level 3 Extended Project Qualification (EPQ) gives sixth-form students in England, Wales and Northern Ireland the opportunity to research and investigate a topic that is important to them. For many, sustainable development and the challenge of climate change may be the motivator that can lead to independent study and develop agency in this field. For more information, read the article by Pearson EPQ examiner Dr John Taylor.[9]

Changes are occurring. There is an exciting new GCSE in Natural History that will be available to teach from September 2025.

> *GCSE in Natural History would reconnect our young people with the natural world around them. Not just because it's fascinating, not just because it's got benefits for mental health, but because we'll need these young people to create a world we can all live in, a vibrant and healthy planet.* –Mary Colwell, Naturalist[10]

Sustainability qualifications in England and Northern Ireland

Could you add a new course to your school or college curriculum to help your students learn about sustainability? Read the mini case study in this section to find out about the courses offered to staff and students at the Eastern Education Group. There are many courses listed on the Regulated Qualifications Framework that can be taught in centres. An internet search of the following list can give you more information about the course level, funding and how to become an approved registered centre:

- **Energy Efficiency and Sustainability:** Entry Level 3 and Level 1 awards from the National Open College Network (NOCN)-approved centres; age 14+.
- **Designing, Engineering and Constructing a Sustainable Built Environment:** Level 1, 2 and 3 awards from The Learning Machine (TLM)-approved centres; age 14–19.
- **Delivering a Sustainability Project:** Entry 3, Level 1 and 2 awards from OCN London-approved centres; age 14–19.
- **Environmental Sustainability:** Level 1 award from AIM Qualifications and Assessment Group-approved centres; age 14+.
- **Sustainability Principles and Project Delivery:** Level 1 award from the Skills and Education Group (SEG)-approved centres; age 14+.
- **Understanding Environmental Sustainability:** Level 2 certificate from Training Qualifications UK (TQUK)-approved centres; age 16+.
- **Global Studies and Sustainability:** Access to HE Diploma from AIM Qualifications and Assessment Group-approved centres; age 16+.
- **Championing Sustainability in the Workplace:** Level 3 certificate from NCFE-approved centres; for Agriculture, Horticulture and Animal Care; age 16+.

> **Things to think about**
>
> Many of the course providers listed above work with schools and colleges. For example, OCN London has qualifications with 'green units' that can be delivered to students aged 14+: https://ocnlondon.org.uk/qualifications/qualifications-with-green-units/.
>
> Have a look at the websites of the other providers listed above. Do they offer courses that would benefit your students? Could your school become an approved centre?

MINI CASE STUDY: EASTERN EDUCATION GROUP, SUFFOLK

The Eastern Education Group includes West Suffolk College, Abbeygate Sixth Form College and One Sixth Form College. Sustainability is embedded across the organisation, with the United Nations SDGs used as a framework to monitor progress across the curriculum and the operational side of the campuses. Introduction to Sustainability workshops are run in many departments, including Early Years, Marketing and Engineering, and there are staff and student sustainability ambassadors who meet regularly to discuss progress.

Specific sustainability education offered at the colleges, for staff, students and local employees, includes:

- Carbon literacy training;
- IEMA level 2–level 4 courses (certified training centre);
- Green skills for educators courses;
- Skills bootcamps.

Whatever their subject, students are encouraged to take part in a range of activities including Sustainable Futures careers fairs and cross-curricular Students Operating Sustainably events. Staff are also encouraged to continue their professional development with Go Green networking to meet people from industry. The Eastern Education Group works closely with the local community too, supporting regular litter picks and primary school events with industry partners.

Reading the **mission and vision** for the Eastern Education Group shows that sustainability is at the heart of everything they do.

Our mission is to integrate sustainability into every aspect of our institution, fostering a culture of environmental stewardship, social responsibility and economic vitality.

[Our vision] To be a beacon of sustainability in education, inspiring a generation of eco-conscious leaders equipped with the knowledge and skills to create a thriving and resilient world for present and future generations.

The achievements of the Eastern Education Group are recognised in the accolades they have received:

- Association of Colleges, Beacon Awards 2024/5 – finalist;
- Green Gown Awards for Student Engagement 2024 – finalist;

Chapter 7: Qualifications in Sustainability

- Bury Free Press Business Awards 2024 – highly commended;
- Suffolk's Creating The Greenest County Awards 2024 – Winner of the Higher Education award.

Creating a culture of sustainable development is essential for fostering meaningful change within any school or college. For staff taking their first steps in this journey, progress with initiatives requires leadership to support and champion efforts at every level. By fostering a shared vision and inspiring both students and colleagues, you can drive impactful action. Being passionate about encouraging positive change is key, as even small, consistent efforts can build lasting momentum for a more sustainable future.

Nina Hart, Group Head of Sustainability

For more information, visit: http://sustainability.easterneducationgroup.ac.uk/.

Chapter 9 gives more practical suggestions to embed sustainable development in both the school/college operations and curriculum.

World of work example: The Institute for Apprenticeships

To commemorate the coronation of King Charles III, case studies for six apprenticeships have been produced highlighting a range of 'green apprenticeships', covering different entry levels and subject areas:

www.instituteforapprenticeships.org/about/real-life-experiences/showcasing-green-apprenticeships/.

How this is useful:

- Allow students to watch the videos and read the biographies of the apprentices.
- For a career area they are interested in, encourage young people to find out about local providers of the course (or similar) and local companies that employ people who do the role.
- If there are no local opportunities, help them to explore where in the country (or world) they could train for this job and enable discussion about how the young person feels about relocating for education/work.

Further education

For those working in a secondary school, it is worth looking in detail at the courses available at your local further education college. Even if these courses are not related to your subject area, this is useful information that you can share with students. Examples include:

- T-level Foundation – Design and Surveying;
- HND Chemistry with Sustainability (two-year course);
- IEMA* Introduction to Net Zero (10-hour self-directed learning course);
- Short online courses about sustainability in specific sectors, such as the beauty sector.

*IEMA is rebranding to the Institute of Sustainability and Environmental Professionals (ISEP).

There may be sector-specific training available, for example, in Scotland; there are Renewable and Energy Efficiency Training Centres located in nine colleges across Scotland, offering a range of courses linked to sustainability and energy.

Things to think about

If you work in a school, you'll be keen to keep up with changes in T levels. The Institute of Apprentices and Technical Education website is a good resource, providing information you can share with young people. By their nature, these *technical* qualifications are closely linked with developments in sustainability.

www.instituteforapprenticeships.org/qualifications/t-levels/t-level-progression-profiles/

Undergraduate courses

This section won't focus on environmental sciences or geography, as it aims to introduce you to the breadth of undergraduate courses that specifically focus on linking sustainability to a subject. Putting the words 'sustainability' and 'sustainable' into the search feature on the UCAS website brings up over 400 undergraduate courses.

There are degree courses linked to specific sectors, such as agriculture, conservation, fashion, business, finance, event management, engineering, product design, architecture and construction. There are also interdisciplinary courses available such as:

- Politics and global sustainability;
- Global development and sustainability;
- Sustainability and social change;
- Economic studies and sustainable development.

Encourage young people to explore courses that intersect their subject interests and sustainability.

Postgraduate study

As with undergraduate degrees, there is a wide range of postgraduate courses available. The possibility of postgraduate study may seem in the distant future for some young people. However, researching this can help them to understand possible education and career pathways and prepare for these – for example, finding out about the prerequisite qualifications and experiences to be able to apply successfully for a master's programme. Potential students apply directly to the university for master's study, and entry requirements can vary depending on the subject. Here are five brief examples to give you an idea of the range of programmes for master's study, with a sustainable theme. (Individual university websites should be explored for further information about the entry requirements, course structure and application process.)

- **MSc Renewable Energy: Technology and Sustainability** at the University of Reading. The entry requirement is a good second-class honours degree or above. The course includes renewable energy systems, carbon management and urban sustainability.
- **MSc Sustainable Food Systems** at UWE Bristol. The entry requirement is a minimum 2:2 honours degree in a related subject, such as geography, biology and food nutrition.
- **MSc Textile Sustainability and Innovation** at the University of Leeds. Entry requirements include a 2:1 or above degree in a related subject such as textiles, business and engineering.
- **MDes Design Innovation** (various courses) with the Glasgow School of Art, based at the Highlands and Islands campus. Entry requirements are usually a good honours degree in any subject. The courses include exploring how new technologies can enhance modern society.
- **MA Environmental Law and Sustainable Development** at SOAS University of London. The usual entry requirement is a relevant degree, 2:1 or above. The course includes optional units such as the human rights of women, law and postcolonial theory and international criminal law.

Things to think about

The Prospects website also has an interesting case study that introduces the University of Manchester's MA Social Change, Environment and Sustainability: www.prospects.ac.uk/case-studies/introducing-ma-social-change-environment-and-sustainability.

What postgrad courses linked to sustainability does your local university offer?

Case study 2, at the end of this chapter, includes the career progression of Luke, who studied sustainability at university and is now a sustainability manager within an organisation. In case study 3 (chapter 8), find out how their degree course led the PEEQUAL entrepreneurs to set up their company.

Sector specific

Many industries are working hard to reduce their impact on the environment and make a positive contribution to society. There is a range of accredited courses linked to sustainability that employees may be able to follow. Here are some examples that may be of interest for young people to be made aware of:

- **Materials:** PIABC is the awarding body supporting the materials industries, for example, minerals, wood and packaging materials: www.piabc.org.uk/.
- **Waste management:** The Chartered Institute of Waste Management (CIWM) has a range of courses supporting those in the sustainability, resources and waste management sector: https://ciwmquals.co.uk/.
- **Environment and sustainability:** The Institute of Sustainability and Environmental Professionals (ISEP), formerly known as the Institute of Environmental Management and Assessment (IEMA), is the professional body supporting those who work within the environment and sustainability sector: www.iema.net/.
- **Construction:** The Supply Chain Sustainability School has a range of courses and self-learning activities that aim to upskill those who work in the built environment sector: www.supplychainschool.co.uk.
- **Science:** My Green Lab supports those working in science to make their working laboratory more sustainable: www.mygreenlab.org/.

This isn't a definitive list of sectors and the related sustainability training. However, it can be used as a starting point in conversations with young people who have an idea of the industry they would like to work in.

World of work example: My Green Lab

My Green Lab is an American non-profit organisation that aims to improve sustainability and reduce waste (energy, water and materials) in the lab. Many research and manufacturing organisations are supporting their employees to become My Green Lab Ambassadors.

How this is useful:

Could your school/college science department work with students to think about how green their lab is (www.mygreenlab.org/how-to-green-lab.html)?

Are there Ambassadors in the UK whom your science department could contact to speak to the students about their work (www.mygreenlab.org/ambassador-program.html)?

 **Things to think about**

For a specific industry, how is it working more sustainably? Are there recognised qualifications that support professional development? Do the associated websites have any case studies or career stories that can be shared with young people?

Conclusion

Why is it important to include a chapter about qualifications in this book?

Young people are interested in the world around them, and some are concerned about the imbalances of power and social justice, economic development and poverty, climate change and biodiversity. Most want to feel empowered to help make the world a better place.

Your curriculum could offer them opportunities to learn about this and show the career progression in specialising in sustainable development within their potential career field, such as law, construction or design. In conversations about further education, teachers can help students appreciate that they can continue to develop their knowledge about sustainability, whatever sector they enter. Enable young people to become their own 'career researcher' and find out about pathways through employment linked to sustainable development.

Remember, there are two big ideas about SDE. This chapter is focused on education ***about*** sustainable development. Chapter 9 will focus on education ***for*** sustainable development. An enriched curriculum that encourages discussion and thinking about sustainable development and the United Nations Sustainable Development Goals could lead a young person to a career purposely linked to sustainable development.

CASE STUDY 2 – LUKE, UNIVERSITY ESTATES SUSTAINABILITY OFFICER

The story in this case study will give you an example of a how an individual's career in sustainability developed.

No two careers are the same, but by learning how Luke developed his interests in school and university, his entry into the workplace as well as the ongoing challenges and successes he has, young people can begin to investigate possible pathways into a career in sustainability.

Setting the scene

Luke has been the Estates Sustainability Officer at a Scottish university for two years.

The university covers multiple sites in Scotland, along with a London campus. The Estates team has wide responsibilities and includes the teams that look after the buildings and day-to-day maintenance, the health and safety team involved in governance, the team that looks after capital projects and strategic investment in university buildings and the sustainability team.

Education

'I grew up in Glasgow and I liked the sciences so picked these subjects at school, as they were always something I wanted to do. My parents didn't go to university, but they encouraged me, and my peers were also thinking about going to university. So, when it came to choosing a degree, I knew I could achieve in science. Initially I wanted to study computer science but panicked when I wrote my personal statement as I realised I still wanted to do chemistry. Even at the point of having to make a decision, I was still unsure about which way to go, but I knew I wanted to make it work. I started an Applied Chemistry degree, which covered chemistry and chemical engineering, at the University of Strathclyde.

'My interest in sustainability started at school. We learnt about renewable energy and technologies in science, and I could see myself being involved in this area in the future. I never had a clear idea of what I could do after my degree but I was interested in postgrad study, either a master's or a PhD. Again, it was a last-minute decision to choose an MSc in Sustainable Energy at the University of Glasgow. This was an interdisciplinary course that included learning about advanced technologies, ethical implications and economic considerations involved in the challenge to combat global climate change. I was really glad I made this decision and chose to commit to studying about renewable energy, as following this course, I knew I wanted to work in this field.'

Early career

'After I completed the master's, I applied for lots of jobs with the large power and renewable energy companies, but I wasn't successful. I got a graduate role with a specialist engineering firm in Manchester that manufactures leak detection equipment for vehicle manufacturers. Although this wasn't focusing on renewable energy, it was in the 'engineering and manufacturing space' and so I was happy with that. My role changed and I focussed more on the supply chains and procurement and worked with the sales and engineering teams, which was useful as I was able to learn what everyone does across the company. This is a good thing about graduate programmes as you can have the opportunity to work with different teams and understand more about the company. The company encouraged me to do a procurement and supply chain diploma to support the job I was doing. This role helped me to understand more about business acumen and administration and has been useful in my current role at the university.

'Things didn't work out in Manchester, so I moved back to Glasgow. I then had the opportunity to do an internship in Spain. It felt like a backward step but this helped me to move into a sustainability-focused EU-funded role, working for a start-up company that was designing charging solutions for electric scooters. This was in the sustainable transport industry, and they were integrating solar panels into pavements across Europe. However, then Covid came along and scuppered things.

'I came back to the UK and quickly managed to get a role with a not-for-profit company that delivers a wide range of energy efficiency and sustainable transport projects, mostly on behalf of the government (e.g. running grant schemes). I worked within the technical team that supported local authorities across Scotland, to help them understand where to locate electric vehicle chargers. We also did technical analysis and background work, helping the local authorities to decarbonise their vehicles and move to electric fleets. This company was based in Edinburgh and I was living in Glasgow and working from home most days, although I did occasionally travel to the Edinburgh office. I wanted a job that didn't involve working from home but was closer to where I live, so I applied for my current job at the university.'

Role at the university

'Sustainable travel and transport are the areas that I was originally most interested in, but the opportunities with this job have helped my knowledge about buildings and estates to grow.

'I work within the Estates team, specifically in sustainability. My line manager is the environmental manager and we have admin support in our team, too. My role is quite broad, I do 'anything green', focusing on the operational side. The main thing I am doing is producing a new organisational sustainability plan for the university. I look at everything we do across the university, finding ways for the organisation to work more sustainably.

- I look at how we operate the buildings and how we can decarbonise the buildings to reduce emissions.
- There is a big focus on travel, and I look at how people interact with the university, how people travel, including business travel for staff. We try to change behaviours to make sure people understand better ways to commute to the university.
- Another area I look at is the university grounds and its management and how we can change practice to make sure the grounds are more biodiverse.
- We look at the catering services in the university and how we can better understand and reduce the impact from our operations here. This might range from changing the food we serve to increasing the number of local suppliers.
- We want to reduce the waste that we produce and improve our performance in recycling and reuse.
- As a public body, the university is subject to strict procurement rules; however, by increasing the sourcing of environmentally friendly goods and services, we can reduce our impact.

'The aim of my role is to drive change in processes, operations and behaviours to reduce emissions and make the university more environmentally friendly.

'Sustainability in the context of the university isn't just reserved to the operational side of things. The university has a strong focus on aligning its research, learning and teaching to the United Nations Sustainable Development Goals. We have a lot of academic expertise across the university in engineering, science and other STEM areas, so we are looking at how to tie these separated, but interlinked, areas together.'

Challenges

'As with many universities, money is our number one challenge. Net zero targets require investment. Many of the big decarbonisation changes involve infrastructure investment and we need to help those who control the budgets to see the bigger picture.

'Knowledge, education and awareness are also a challenge. The sustainability team is still learning and I'm not an expert and, like many people, sometimes I have imposter syndrome. We are explaining things to people who may not understand the technicalities or jargon as readily as we do. We need to 'sell the benefits' and help people to break it down and understand why we are doing this and what the benefits are to individuals, the university and community, and the planet. Travel is a good example of one area that I have been working on to improve. Changing behaviours, to encourage people to get the bus or train instead of driving, can be a challenge. At a personal level, sometimes people don't want to make those changes and bringing them along on the journey can be difficult. So, a 'hearts and minds' approach is best, helping people to understand why the changes are important and needed.

'Most of the team is based at the university's main campus, and sometimes we don't get as much time at the other campuses as we would like to and sometimes it's easy to lose track of what's going on at other campuses. Our scope and influence across each site varies quite a lot. Our main focus is at certain campuses, which we own and control directly. A smaller campus, with about 300 students, has recently been co-located with a local college, and we keep in touch with their sustainability team. Another site is mainly for international, postgraduate students and is two floors in a big building. We're working to grow our partnerships with colleagues at these campuses.'

Next steps for Luke

'The work of many of my colleagues is focussed on buildings and estates, from an architectural, management or technical point of view. Learning how the building works, the 'hands on' stuff', is important to me. If I understand better how the buildings work and how the whole entity functions, I can sell the sustainability better to others. For example, we have older and newer buildings that have different levels of efficiency. People want the heating on and the windows open, so we need to know how to heat the buildings, how we change the windows and insulate better. Knowledge about how the building works is part of carbon management.'

Advice for people interested in a career in sustainability

'Although there are lots of new degree courses that are interdisciplinary and include sustainability, any STEM degree will give you the problem-solving experience that can be useful for a technical career in sustainability. Study a subject that you enjoy, as picking a more conventional degree, such as chemical engineering, doesn't mean you won't experience developments linked to your subject; things will cross over and you'll learn about sustainability.

'The range of postgrad courses linked to sustainability is growing, from more technical/engineering to those focusing on sustainability and humanitarian issues. A simple way to think about it is how much maths is involved! There are different levels of flexibility in different master's programmes, and in some you can pick topics to study, such as technical units that involve a lot of data and maths and ethics units looking at the issues connected with environmental sustainability. In these classes you might meet students who did different types of undergrad degrees, such as sciences and engineering or sustainable development and social sciences.

'It takes time to become an expert in an area of sustainability, and there is lots that you can learn about the workplace in general that will help you to have an impact in an organisation. When you are in employment, take the opportunity to learn about business administration and management; it will come in useful when you are working in an organisation. Understanding contracts and economics is good bits of knowledge to have and will be useful in whatever you do.'

And finally . . .

'Working in sustainability affords you the opportunity to learn lots across a vast sector which is continually growing.

'I'm motivated by being able to make a small difference at a local level and by being able to see new technologies in action.'

Chapter 8
Rising to the challenge

> Environmental and social factors often compete with economic factors, but whenever there is a problem, there is always a solution.

Introduction

With any 'big issue' (which sustainability undoubtedly is), there are tensions. There will be people and organisations leading the change, followers embracing the new direction, neutral folk who want to hear both sides of the argument and sceptics who are reluctant to see the need for change.

Producing a net zero economy and finding long-term solutions to local and global problems will take time and effort. There are potential conflicts to be resolved and people to convince. This chapter will take a range of issues in turn and identify ways in which we can help young people, and ourselves, to understand these and see the need for finding solutions.

If you're reading this book, you are probably interested in people, their career and the planet. There will be tensions and ethical issues for you to acknowledge and address, too. Therefore, we will consider ethical frameworks you can use, to ensure that young people are encouraged to have autonomy and agency in their decision-making.

One of the biggest problems in career development work is that there is no common agreement on the language and terms used. We have a jingle-jangle of nomenclature! This is when the same terms are used for different things (jingle) or different terms are used for the same thing (jangle)! Marciniak, Johnston, Steiner and Hirschi (2022) argue that it is the interdisciplinary approach to conceptualising and researching career development that leads to the fragmentation of the language.[1]

Career development academics are currently researching what 'green guidance' actually is, looking at how concepts are linked, such as consumption (using up the planet's resources), environmental and social impact (how biodiversity and society are affected) and the labour market (jobs available now and in the future). You can keep up to date with some of the research on websites such as: www.green-guidance.eu/.

Does it matter what terms and definitions we use? Understanding the fundamental components is arguably more important than buzz terms. However, if you can encourage your school/college to use the same definitions for terms such as career, skills, green jobs and green skills, you'll help your staff and students navigate the complex concepts of career development and sustainable development with more confidence.

Political thinking

We're off track

In July 2024, the UK's Climate Change Committee reported that although the UK has decreased its carbon emissions (mainly due to the energy sector reforms), we are not on track to reduce emissions in 2030 by 68% compared to 1990 levels, the first net zero target the UK set during the Paris Agreement in 2016.[2] Other sectors, such as industry, transport, buildings, waste and agriculture, need to make rapid progress to embrace low-carbon technologies and reduce their carbon emissions significantly.[2] Our reduced demand for gas as a source of electricity in buildings is a success story; however, the list of measures that are off track makes depressing reading:

- Electric car and van sales;
- Heat pump installations;
- Offshore wind operational capacity;
- New woodland creation and peatland restoration.[2]

These are topics that we can discuss with young people, but career support should remain unbiased. Many families might be considering buying an electric car, and some households might be investigating having a heat pump installed. Wind turbines are on the curriculum in science lessons, with students learning how they work and the issues surrounding wind farms. There may be less discussion about planting trees and the environmental benefits of peatland, but perhaps you can help to address this.

Chapter 8: Rising to the Challenge

Things to think about

Create time in the curriculum (careers and subject) for the measures above to be discussed:

- How does this relate to a young person's day-to-day life?
- What sectors, careers and jobs are linked to this topic?

Try to allow space for exploring the facts as well as more emotive discussions.

The blog written by a young person for the Young Minds website gives the lived experience of coping with climate anxiety and tips you can share with students: www.youngminds.org.uk/young-person/blog/how-to-cope-with-climate-anxiety/.

Things to think about

When facilitating discussions, things to bear in mind are some of the challenges and barriers:

- Climate debate is a complex topic; try to avoid the binary of 'good' or 'bad'.
- Climate anxiety exists and particularly affects young people.[3]
- Being interested in climate change can be seen as political and activist. Some students may be excited by this, and others are reluctant to be considered 'extreme'.
- We need a 'Just Transition', with fairness and equity for all. For some families, having a heat pump and electric car is out of financial reach or the infrastructure is unavailable.

Money, money, money

Progress and money are closely linked together. Here are three examples that are useful to share with young people, in terms of being a consumer, future employment opportunities and progress towards the UK achieving net zero by 2050.

Data – Who owns the data, how is the data shared, how is the data protected, who can afford to buy the data and what can be gleaned from the data if the right person is looking at it? Many organisations collect and store data about their customers, for example, via a loyalty scheme. Primarily, this data is used by the retailer to improve sales and increase revenue. But what are the other uses of the data? Using grocery retail as an example, how could the data gained from a supermarket loyalty app be of use to the farmer, food manufacturer or a local food bank charity? Could the data help to reduce waste from field to fork? Could (and should) the data be used to inform policy and improve the nation's health? There are implications about the energy use of large data centres. See chapter 5 for more information.

Examples of jobs using data that will become more prominent include data protection lawyers, data scientists and procurement managers.

Carbon trading – This is a complex topic and one that young people should be aware of. For some organisations, reducing their carbon dioxide emissions is a slow process. A whole new 'carbon market' has grown since the Kyoto Protocol of 1997, and the 2015 Paris Agreement set out international carbon dioxide emission goals.[4] In the UK, there are regulated cap-and-trade schemes that 'cap' the amount of greenhouse gas emitted by sectors and allow companies to 'trade' their leftover allowances.[5] Then there is carbon offsetting. This is when organisations 'offset' their carbon emissions by paying into a scheme that reduces atmospheric greenhouse gases. (An example young people may have heard of is when booking a flight with an additional fee option for carbon offsetting.) There are four main ways carbon offsetting is done:

1. Investing in renewable energy schemes;
2. Capturing the methane released in industrial processes;
3. Nature restoration projects, such as tree planting and coastal marine ecosystem development;
4. Mechanical carbon dioxide capture, also known as sequestration.[4]

Trading in carbon credits (one credit equals one tonne of CO_2) and carbon offsetting can form part of a company's strategy to reduce its carbon footprint, but there are ethical dilemmas with this, too. Could trading in carbon credits and offsetting just prolong the time it takes for a company to decarbonise? Are people living in the nature restoration area consulted and involved in the project? How do we know if a company is using its carbon offsetting schemes as a way to hide its lack of decarbonising progress (greenwashing[6])?

Examples of jobs linked to the carbon market that will become more prominent include: low-carbon business adviser, carbon emissions analyst, carbon specialist, environmental solicitor, carbon trader and marketing.

Chapter 8: Rising to the Challenge

 World of work example: Ecologi and Make It Wild

Ecologi (formally known as Offset Earth) is a UK company with a 'mission to inspire and empower businesses to accelerate global climate action'.

Make It Wild, also based in the UK, is a 'multi-award winning family business creating space for nature'.

How this is useful:

Encourage young people to be critical thinkers when they explore a company's website, for example:

https://ecologi.com/why-ecologi/trust-through-transparency

www.makeitwild.co.uk/testimonials-from-business-partners

- What are the key points being made (such as arguments and claims)?
- What is the evidence? How strong is this evidence and what is the source?
- Having read the information, what are *your* views?

Extracting oil – Companies in the UK are continuing to extract gas and oil, mainly from the North Sea, and over 120,000 people are directly or indirectly employed in the sector.[7] The move away from using fossil fuels as an energy source is contentious in regions that rely on the sector for employment. New 'green' jobs are developing (see chapter 4), but there are concerns about the impact on local communities if there are large job losses linked to a reduction in fossil fuel extraction. However, despite the UK moving towards green energy, we still need oil! Refining crude oil forms materials that are required in the manufacture of many well-known products, including plastics, rubber, paints, fabrics, cleaning and beauty products, medical devices such as heart valves, furniture finish, sporting equipment and agricultural chemicals, such as fertilisers.[8]

 Interesting fact

Lubricants are important in industrial processes and car engines to reduce damage to parts of machinery due to friction. Traditionally, lubricants are made from crude oil. Many manufacturing companies are switching to 'eco-friendly' alternatives made out of materials such as plant oils and graphite. Different materials have different properties, so it is important to consider the temperature, pressure and environment the lubricant is used in.[9]

Things to think about

Society needs to consider how it manufactures, uses, recycles and disposes of plastics. A Plastic Planet has a single goal: 'to ignite and inspire the world to turn off the plastic tap'. How can you help young people to be critical users of plastic products? What do you need to change in your work environment to facilitate this? What examples can your students give of plastic usage being reduced? What replacement materials are used instead, and how were these solutions created? Encourage a discussion about when it may be appropriate to use 'single-use' plastics, for example, in healthcare. What innovation would be required to reduce this 'necessary' use of plastic?

For more information visit: https://aplasticplanet.com/ and https://plasticfree.com/.

What about jobs?

Chapters 3 and 4 discussed green jobs. The threat of machines taking over and traditional roles becoming obsolete is a concern for many, and teachers and career professionals must acknowledge this. Young people will be hearing about the changing job market at home and on the news, and we can help them to put things into perspective. A few contentious issues are discussed below, some you may be aware of and others that may be useful for you to consider:

- **Minority groups** are still under represented in many sectors and job roles. As many science, technology and engineering sectors are driving us towards net zero, *STEM Careers* (2nd edition) has useful links to organisations supporting under-represented groups working in STEM.
- The workforce has always needed to **upskill** and learn new skills. Just think about the changes in your lifetime. Digital skills are at the forefront, and this is not always an area that schools excel at but create opportunities to support young people to develop theirs.
- Skills have become a big topic in education, but have you heard of **'capitals'** (briefly mentioned in chapter 1 and discussed further in chapter 3)? There are many, and combing through academic literature adds to the list: for example, employability, economic, social, scholastic, cultural, health and science capital. Young people can develop their employability, and *how they perceive their employability*, by being aware of their levels of individual capital and how external factors can affect their capital. This can help them to successfully transition from education to the labour market.[10]
- Interesting work from Nesta, an innovation agency, looked at the skills listed in over 40 million UK job adverts and, using machine

learning, constructed clusters of skills in a hierarchy. **Social work and caregiving** is the sector with the most demanded skills, and those skills are cooking, caregiving, care planning, social work and home management.[11] This supports the 2024 data from the UK government about the occupations in demand.[12] The country needs people to do these jobs. How do we help young people to see them as rewarding careers?

- **Sickness absence** from work has become a national crisis, and the number of economically inactive adults has been a problem for many years. This is not just due to Covid. As a society, we need to rethink how we prevent and solve long-term ill health. (See chapter 3 for more discussion about mental health and work.) Employers have a part to play, but how can teachers and career professionals contribute to a young person developing their psychological and health capitals, to be able to manage their health and well-being as adults?

Education

Are you ready?

In Scotland, Education for Sustainable Development is explicit throughout the Professional Standards for Teachers underpinned by the 'Learning for Sustainability' network, yet in England, there is no mention of sustainable development education (SDE) in the Teacher Standards. Both teaching and career development work always take place within political and societal contexts. Sustainable development is an emotive topic, so if there isn't a statutory guideline for your circumstances, be driven by data and scientific facts and help young people become critical thinkers.

Careers professionals and teachers need to have confidence in delivering sustainability and careers programmes. If staff have a lack of knowledge, is there time for CPD (see chapter 7) and perhaps to visit local employers and find out what their sustainability problems are (e.g. recruiting and retaining staff, reducing carbon emissions and working more sustainably, developing solutions and products)? If you know what your local employers' priorities are, you can begin to address this in your careers education programme.

Engaging stakeholders (students, teachers, parents, employers and the school's senior leadership team) in the design of the programme can help it to be meaningful and purposeful to all. But this leads to tensions: Is there time allocated to develop and evaluate this? Is there time in the curriculum to deliver this? Are objectives agreed upon and aligned with individual stakeholder groups' priorities? How do you make sustainable connections with industry and collaborate for the benefit of education and employer, year on year?

Things to think about

Can you find inspiring role models that your young people can relate to? For example, female trade apprentices, male healthcare workers, academic researchers and innovators.

Chapter 9 will offer strategies for schools to embed and make space for programmes such as WWF-UK Sustainable Futures and Manchester Good Work, with ideas for practical delivery across the curriculum.

Supporting young people

The three big themes running through this book, sustainability and careers, having a sustainable career and SDE are underpinned by two perspectives:

- Sustainable development, for the benefit of the planet (environment and society).
- Having a sustainable career, for the benefit of the individual.

Be clear about the purpose of the activity. That is, the work you do with young people, i.e., a specific activity, a longer programme or the underlying themes in your classroom. Is the outcome to help your students understand more about how their behaviour and career can impact the planet? Or are you focusing on helping young people develop career management skills to enable them to have a long and fulfilling working life? The activity or programme can have both objectives, but be clear that you, the staff, using the resources and the students understand them.

Chapter 2 discusses why the United Nations Sustainable Development Goals are important and most governments in the world have signed up to the Paris Agreement (to reduce carbon pollution and become net zero by 2050). Careers practitioners and teachers can have a part to play, as individuals have an impact on society, the environment and the planet. However, we must work in an ethical manner and in the best interests of the young person. The Career Development Institute has a Code of Ethics to guide practice that can be useful for teachers, too: give impartial information and enable students to develop their agency and autonomy so that they can make their own informed decisions.[13] (See the suggested further reading below and chapter 1 for more information about climate anxiety and counselling.)

Careers education should broaden disadvantaged groups' choices. In 2021, research from the Social Mobility Commission highlighted that four in five adults believe there is a large gap between the social classes and 39% think it is harder for people from less advantaged families to move up in British society.[14] Could learning entrepreneurial skills be useful? The US-based

'Entrepreneurial mindset' framework is innovative and creative.[15] However, this can be considered as a privileged way of working, so be mindful of this when working with young people.

Disruptors

There are some great examples of entrepreneurs disrupting the status quo and forcing change. Often termed 'disruptors', these innovators challenge the accepted ways of doing things and offer alternative solutions; think about Uber and Airbnb. Although these two organisations are global successes, their dominance is not always welcome. However, explore their websites to see ways they are trying to make a positive difference – for example, Uber's commitment to reduce carbon emissions and plastic waste and Airbnb providing emergency accommodation during crisis events.

If the general ideas of sustainable development (for either the environment or society) are at the heart of the motivation of the entrepreneur, the results can be inspiring. The three values of fashion retailer Lucy and Yak are creativity, community and comfort. They only use sustainable fabrics and encourage customers to exchange their old 'yaks' for money off their next purchase. The second-hand clothes are then resold in stores. Other, larger, high-street fashion retailers are following suit; for example, Primark have their 'Love it for longer' campaign, encouraging customers to learn how to repair clothes! Food manufacturer Ben & Jerry's website states, 'We love making ice cream – but using our business to make the world a better place gives our work its meaning.' With product, economic and social missions, sustainability linked to prosperity is at the heart of the company.

Sometimes an innovative idea needs a helping hand. Global initiatives can drive change, and some interesting examples to share with young people include:

- Royal Society's Global Challenges Research Fund;
- Earthshot Prize;
- Challenge Works (a Nesta enterprise);
- Gates Foundation grants.

Why this is useful for young people to know about? The skills of entrepreneurship are probably already being developed in your school/college. Students may be involved in science, STEM and engineering clubs that encourage creativity and design, possibly taking part in national competitions such as Big Bang, Teen Tech, First Tech Robotics Challenge and F1 in Schools. Inspirational stories about young people finding solutions to problems can help them to learn about different pathways such as academic research and business development. Read the PEEQUAL case study at the end of this chapter, to find out how two university graduates are revolutionising toilets at festivals! More sources for stories include:

- https://startups.co.uk/startups-100/
- https://justentrepreneurs.co.uk/
- www.smeweb.com/top-100-young-british-entrepreneurs-shaping-future-of-uk-economy/
- https://www.enterprisenation.com/

Global health organisation BUPA runs an eco-disruptive programme that invests in innovation. This pioneering scheme promotes their staff development too, by encouraging employees to scout for start-up companies that have innovative healthcare solutions and mentor the participants through the programme. Read more about their work on the BUPA website: www.bupa.com/impact/action/eco-disruptive.

World of work example: Colorfix

Synthetic fabric dyes usually contain heavy metals that can pollute the environment. Colorfix, started by two biologists, use cutting-edge biological techniques to provide natural-based pigments to the textile industry. Colorfix was an Earth Shot Prize UK nominee in 2023: https://colorifix.com/our-story/.

How this is useful:

- Encourage biology teachers to use the information from the Colorfix website during class discussions about genetic modification.
- Give students time to explore the Earthshot website, including the winners and finalists: https://earthshotprize.org/.
  - What challenges are they addressing?
  - What is their solution?
  - Is there a story that relates to the student's interests?

Conclusion

Driving the change required to reduce the impact of climate change and social injustice isn't easy. Governments and organisations, at local and global levels, will need to find ways to bring society and the workforce along to produce a just, net zero economy. Organisations and individuals will be required to embrace change, and adults who support young people have a part to play. To adopt a SAS saying: let's leave no person behind.

Education takes place within a political space, with teachers and career professionals helping young people to balance scientific evidence and public

Chapter 8: Rising to the Challenge

opinion to form their views. Acknowledging the tensions and creating space for debate is necessary to make everyone, staff and students, informed and feel involved in the discussion about sustainable development and having a sustainable career.

Chapter 9 will delve deeper into the strategies you can use in your school and college to develop a *sustainable* careers education programme that helps young people develop a greater understanding of their place in the world, both now and throughout their adult lives. Chapter 9 will also highlight activities and resources that can help you to teach about sustainable development and enrich your career education programme. (See chapter 7 for specific qualifications, for educators and young people, about sustainability.)

CASE STUDY 3 – PEEQUAL, AN ENTREPRENEURIAL COMPANY

This case study will give you an example of how two individuals developed their entrepreneurial mindset, identified a gap, developed a product and went on to form a company.

By learning more about entrepreneurs, young people can understand how an individual's values and behaviours can be focussed to help them develop a product to market in a sustainable way.

Disrupting the norm

Anyone who attends festivals and outdoor events knows that queuing for the cubicle loo can be time-consuming and takes you away from the action of the event. For years, many events have provided urinals for men, cutting down their waiting time.

But what about women who just need a quick pee?

About the company

PEEQUAL is on a pee-equality mission. They provide innovative female urinals that cut down the toilet queuing time for women at festivals, marathons and other outdoor events. Taken from their website, the company values are:

- Passionate: We are here to leave a mark, change attitudes and drive change for women.
- Bold: We shake things up and never shy away from challenging the status quo.

- Sustainable: We are committed to making a positive impact on the environment.
- Innovative: We are explorers constantly seeking new opportunities and markets.
- Playful: We champion the fun and creativity throughout our work.
- Principled: We exist to deliver equality and excellence for women.

About the co-founders

Company co-founders Hazel McShane and Amber Probyn both had a natural problem-solving flare when they were children, enjoying the creative freedom to build and make things. They met at the University of Bristol on the four-year integrated master's degree courses, Hazel studying Physics and Innovation and Amber studying Anthropology and Innovation.

Following an open day at the University of Bristol, Amber knew she wanted to be on the Innovation Programme after becoming inspired when hearing about the course. She set herself this goal and worked hard at school, successfully gaining a place on the course. Meanwhile, Hazel's route to university involved having a gap year. At 18 she bought and renovated a van and explored Europe, getting as far as Montenegro. After returning to the UK, Hazel started university, thinking the Innovation Programme was a unit in the physics degree and not actually a main part of the master's qualification!

During the fourth year of the course the pair collaborated on a project to 'solve a real-world problem'. Hazel previously worked in festivals and experienced the female toilet queues that have become normalised, as we all expect and accept them. Why hadn't this problem been solved before? Had the taboo of innovation in this area hindered exploring the problem? Hazel pitched the idea to Amber, and the pair had a natural synergy with Amber's understanding of anthropology and Hazel's scientific approach.

Inventing the women's urinal

The pair started with exploring the problem of female toilet queues and the taboo of discussing women peeing. Speaking and consulting with women led to the solution. They realised that they could design and create a product that would reduce the peeing time and therefore the queuing time. Initially, Amber and Hazel used cardboard to make 3D models of their first designs. They even sewed old bouncy castle material in one of the iterations of the design.

Just after the first pandemic lockdown, even though they didn't feel ready, the pair were encouraged by an adviser to 'just go for it' and take their prototype to a Covid-safe event at Bristol Comedy Gardens. This design was made out of wood they had found in a hedge and spray-painted scrap metal. The measurements were wrong (too small!) but the women at the event had so many things to say, giving Amber and Hazel the energy to take this further.

During trials, they let women explore the PEEQUAL and tried to get unbiased feedback. Women were involved at every stage of the development: how do they pee? (sit on a toilet or hover above the seat?), what height should the walls of the structure be? (to hide faces while peeing). Women squat differently to pee and so the pedestal had to be designed with a curve to prevent splashback occurring for all users. The urine collector is gravity-fed, so no 'blue-flush' chemicals or electricity are required.

They charged those first customers, even though the design was still a prototype. This meant they could get proper, unbiased feedback from the client (i.e. the event organiser) as well as the women using their urinals.

The important features of the urinal are that this is a safe space for women to pee, is hygienic as it doesn't involve the user touching any surface and is easy to keep clean with minimum need to use water. The design is flexible, as the units are 'flat-packed' and can be assembled to be stand-alone, arranged in a circle, semi-circle or a line.

Working in a sustainable way

Early feedback about their unique urinal was positive, and Hazel and Amber realised that to reach as many women as possible, they needed a design suitable for mass scale up. While making something new, they decided to also limit their impact on the environment.

The company is based in Hereford, and currently the urinals are manufactured in nearby Somerset. They wanted to avoid using 'virgin plastic' in the manufacturing process, and the materials used in the urinals include a biopolymer made from sugar cane and recycled plastics collected from the world's oceans.

The biggest carbon impact of PEEQUAL is transporting the urinals. They are delivered to the events on an articulated lorry and because of the design, they can be transported 'flat pack', ensuring three times more urinals are stacked on the lorry compared to usual portable toilet cubicles. Less lorries transporting the required urinals means that less fuel is used and therefore less carbon dioxide released.

Urine can be used for so many different things, from generating electricity to fertiliser. The urinal is designed for pee (not poo) so that the urine can be collected, in order to be converted into something useful. Around Bristol there are lots of start-up hubs, so at first Hazel and Amber talked to lots of different companies that could potentially use the urine. Eventually a company approached them to buy the urine and process it to make fertiliser for farms across the South West of England.

The challenges of being an entrepreneur

Developing a product costs money. As students, Hazel and Amber didn't know much about how to access money, but on the Innovation Programme they learnt about different ways to access grants, for example, the HSBC-run Grant for a Grand, and there were pockets of money available from the University of Bristol for developing and growing an idea. Winning some of this money actually allowed Amber and Hazel to afford the fuel to deliver the PEEQUAL units to some of their first customers!

Manufacturing on a large scale involves hundreds of thousands of pounds, and grants of this size aren't available. So Amber and Hazel had to find alternative funds. They went on mini-business courses, such as Accelerators, to learn about how to grow a business and find investors. They raised money via private equity investment (think 'Dragon's Den'!) and participated in the London School of Economics Impact Fund, for those working towards the United Nations Sustainable Development Goals.

Fundraising for a business based on women using the toilet was challenging at times, with potential male investors laughing and not taking them seriously. Being co-founders helped Hazel and Amber as they were not alone and kept each other going in the search for 'angels' (large investors).

As the company grows bigger, the production of the urinals will need to increase. Ocean plastic waste is used as one of the materials for their product, and finding a UK company able to continue this, at scale, is not easy; therefore, they are exploring manufacturing in the EU, as long as the products are transported over road, not air, to minimise carbon production.

The company is customer driven – manufacturing these urinals is not cheap and so for a customer hiring them, it may cost more than conventional cubical toilets. But some customers *do* want a more sustainable product and *are* willing to pay this, to help as many women as possible at their event have a safe space for a quick pee.

Chapter 8: Rising to the Challenge

The benefit of university for a budding entrepreneur

During the 'innovation' part of the master's degree, Hazel and Amber learnt about solving a problem and the methodologies of how to create change. They were taught to be as divergent as possible and take inspiration from everywhere before settling on a solution.

The university's public relations department had sent out communications prior to the Bristol Comedy Gardens event, and this led to a crazy media explosion, with the *Times*, BBC, *Cosmopolitan Japan* contacting them! From then, Hazel and Amber knew that they were onto something with this idea and that they 'couldn't put it to bed'.

Learning about testing procedures and designing a product helped them to look for the truth in the feedback, to not just accept a 'yes' about the design but to understand *why* a user gave that feedback.

Get involved with PEEQUAL

Visit the website to look at the PEEQUAL urinal design and find out more about the company: www.peequal.com/.

As well as paid temporary and permanent roles, the company has volunteering opportunities at the events they attend. Volunteers can develop their skills in working with the public, gain experience of working at events, such as festivals, and help women to avoid the long toilet cubicle queues.

Things to think about

When she was younger, Amber knew she wanted to start a company; Hazel on the other hand didn't know what an entrepreneur was but she wanted to solve a real-life problem. Young people learn about enterprise within the careers curriculum, and it is important for them to hear different stories about starting a company. As well as the 'grow a pound' types of activities, allow time for students to:

- Learn about innovation and explore the courses available at university, linked to subject areas they are passionate about.
- Find out about support programmes for 'start-ups', for example, with the local authority, university or national banks: www.natwest.com/business/business-services/entrepreneur-accelerator.html.
- Meet local entrepreneurs who have set up their own business. (You can find people at local business networking meetings.)

Chapter 9
Sustainability and career education

> Education leads to knowledge and knowledge can lead to power; let's empower our young people by putting and keeping sustainability in the career education curriculum.

Introduction

There are three main themes throughout this book:

1. **Sustainability and careers:** The types of 'green jobs' and skills required for sectors to reduce their greenhouse gas emissions and encourage nature restoration.

2. **A sustainable career:** Preparing young people for a sustainable career that gives them decent work prepares them for lifelong learning and doesn't negatively affect their mental health.

3. **Sustainable development education (SDE):** Teaching *about* and teaching *for* sustainable development.

A new idea is now introduced – that a school/college *itself* should have *sustainable* sustainability and career education programmes that are well planned, meet the needs of its community, are progressive and reproducible.

This chapter draws on the ideas previously discussed to help teachers and career professionals develop a strategy to help their young people prepare for a successful and long career that embraces sustainability. Stefania Giannini, Assistant Director-General for Education at UNESCO, states, 'Education for Sustainable Development can provide the knowledge, awareness and action that empower people to transform themselves and transform societies.'[1] By providing a road map, UNESCO hopes that education can continue to contribute towards a 'more just and sustainable world' through 'individual and societal transformation'.[1]

Frameworks that can be used to guide delivery will be discussed in this chapter, as will strategies to ensure your SDE curriculum is relevant to your school/college stakeholders. The young person is at the heart of this transformational change, and guidance to promote a whole school approach that empowers educators to put the student at the centre will be shared. Practical examples of activities that can be delivered in the school and college setting will also be explored, with advice about how to make these events repeatable and sustainable.

The chapter is followed by a case study from Bedford Academy about the sustainability work the school is doing. There is also a short section about the Department for Education's Sustainability and Climate Change Strategy and practical advice about how schools can develop their Climate Action Plans.

> Although this definition of SDE is rather old, it is still useful:
>
> '... enable students to think creatively and critically, to solve problems and to make a difference for the better ... It should develop their awareness, understanding and respect for the environments in which they live and secure their commitment to sustainable development at a personal, local, national and global level'. (DfEE/QCA, 1999, The National Curriculum: Handbook for secondary teachers in England)

Frame it!

Properly delivered, SDE helps learners to develop the skills, knowledge, values and behaviours to make the world a better place, for themselves and future generations. But how do you weave this into your curriculum in a coherent way that is understood by all, from senior leaders and teachers to students and their parents?

Frameworks can be used to keep you focused and can help you design a curriculum that enhances learning outcomes. Three suggested sources for frameworks for SDE are:

1. The 17 Sustainable Development Goals (SDGs)[2]
From decent work to human rights and environmental issues, there is something for everyone in the 17 SDGs. Are sustainability issues integrated into the teaching and learning in all subject areas? Do your students have the opportunity to explore all 17 goals and the associated targets across the curriculum? What are a student's next steps once they have interrogated a goal? How are students supported to further explore a goal that aligns with

Chapter 9: Sustainability and Career Education

their values and interests? Do students learn about global opportunities for people with skills that are in demand? If you are a career professional, do you consider using the SDGs during your discussions with a young person?

Dr Inge Hill, Lecturer in Entrepreneurship at the Open University Business School, suggests that this framework alone isn't enough to integrate the SDGs into the curriculum.[3] Although her writing is focused on higher education courses, it can inform using the SDGs in secondary school subject teaching:

- As a school, agree on the definition of 'green skills' and sustainability.
- Show students the 'bigger picture' of how your subject can help to address specific SDGs.
- Within each topic for a subject, identify which SDG and targets are the most appropriate to address.
- Find, or develop, resources that will help you to deliver the topic linked to the SDG and target.

Each change of mind is a contribution to achieving the SDGs! Mind-by-mind we can achieve the system change needed to live more sustainably. (Dr Inge Hill)[3]

For more information about how education can help society to meet the SDGs, read the Education for Sustainable Development Roadmap: https://unesdoc.unesco.org/ark:/48223/pf0000374802.

2. The CDI Career Development Framework[4]

The CDI has created a framework that is useful for career leaders planning their careers programme, accessible for teachers delivering career education within their lessons and career practitioners during guidance meetings.

The framework can help students develop the skills, knowledge and attitudes to be able to positively manage their career throughout their life. Does your curriculum offer learning opportunities to engage with the six learning areas identified in the framework? (See chapter 2 for more information about each learning area.) Are subject teachers, career professionals and pastoral staff involved in delivering this? Do all teachers 'see the bigger picture' (sixth learning area) and encourage their students to, as well? Does your programme encourage young people to engage with local, national and international news so that they know what is affecting the world of work? For example, policies affecting specific sectors and new technologies driving change in the workplace.

3. Environmentally sustainable career guidance[5]

If you are a career practitioner you'll know that career development is an important field within the discussion of climate change, environmental

Table 9.1. Dimsits and Hooley's five dimensions for environmentally sustainable career guidance[5]

Dimension	What this means	Using this in education
Affective	Feeling empathy with nature and connecting your career with the world (environment, nature, society).	Use nature as the setting for learning. Allow empathy and emotions with discussions about the environment. For 'nature connectedness research', visit: www.derby.ac.uk/research/themes/zero-carbon/zero-carbon-nbs-research-centre/nature-connectedness-research-group/. Use Hope-Action Theory interventions in discussions about career: (https://hopeactioninventory.com/about/).
Social-ecological	Recognising that our careers are connected to nature and to other people and that you need to build solidarity to underpin your career.	Group and project work. Learning about local communities (human, plant and animal). Working with local communities to effect positive change.
Educational	Building understanding about careers and sustainability to underpin career development	Human activities impact the natural world – explore connections between the world of work and different sectors and the climate and biodiversity crisis. Explore how careers can contribute to the transition to net zero. Link to labour market information: the skills and jobs that address environmental sustainability.
Transformational	Imagining and inventing the world as we would like it to be as we think about and develop our career.	Scenario building for a desired future. Imaging a vocation that offers hope (for the individual, community or environment). Working creatively and collaboratively to make change happen. Inventing and problem-solving solutions (write a mission statement – see the box in this chapter).
Political-ideological	Recognising that careers take place in a political environment and that we can change the world through our careers.	Explore the possible conflicts between the individual's well-being and the sustainability ideology. (See chapter 8 for discussions about tension and conflict.) Encourage students to critically interrogate new and dominant ideologies. Enable the development of career values (without teachers imposing their values and positions).

damage and depletion of biodiversity, but concepts such as 'green' and sustainability can be vague, as the connection between an individual's and society's consumption and the impact on the environment is not always clear.

The research of Miriam Dimsits and Tristram Hooley delivered in a presentation at the 2024 NICEC conference on sustainability and career gives us a detailed definition of environmentally sustainable career guidance (see box below) and five dimensions that could be used as a framework in education (see Table 9.1).[5] This framework can be used holistically to consider SDE as well as guidance; for example, what are the school/college's strategies and policies? How do these dimensions fit and therefore support them? (See the box in this chapter about how Action Learning Sets can be used to make a change in the way SDE is delivered.)

A definition of environmentally sustainable career guidance

Environmentally sustainable career guidance empowers individuals, groups and collectives to develop their lives and careers in ways that do not compromise the ability of other people nor future generations to meet their needs. It recognises that human beings are a part of nature which is valuable in its own right, and that all life, particularly the life of the most vulnerable, is threatened by a growing climate crisis, the depletion of biodiversity and other environmental damage caused by human action.

Environmentally sustainable career guidance is a pedagogic intervention which builds individual and community capacity to analyse, respond to, and address social, environmental and career problems whilst supporting people to build a good life for themselves and others. Fundamentally it aims to stimulate people's imagination and empower them to find their way to a better life and a sustainable world.

(Dimsits and Hooley, 2024)[5]

What does this mean?

- We should all seek a way to live and have our career without harming the planet now and for future generations.
- People are a part of nature and are interdependent on it.
- The effects of climate change are often experienced most acutely by the most vulnerable people and other living things.
- Environmentally sustainable career guidance teaches people how they can respond to, and solve, environmental problems through their career and by working with others.
- A key aim of career guidance should be to inspire and excite people to imagine and create a better life for themselves and others and contribute to a more sustainable world.

Sustainable Careers

Things to think about

What career education frameworks does your school/college already use?

How easily could the frameworks listed above be adapted for use in your setting?

More information about: Action Learning Sets

Use the Action Learning Set model as a way to:

- work with colleagues to plan transformational change in your school/college, putting SDE at the heart of your community;
- structure some student activities in the classroom, with teachers and young people discussing problems, exploring resources and planning actions.

Consider Hooley and Dimsits' five dimensions for environmentally sustainable career guidance[4] (Table 9.1).[5] How could these dimensions be useful in an educational setting when planning activities for young people?

See the resources section at the end of the book for further reading about Action Learning Sets.

Make it relevant

You'll have more success with introducing and maintaining SDE and sustainable career education and guidance if it is relevant to your school/college and setting.

- Do your programmes (SDE and careers education) meet the needs of your students and local community, and do all staff understand this purpose?
- Do you work with your stakeholders (parents, young people, local colleges and universities, local authority and local employers), learning what the local priorities are, in terms of the workforce, environmental projects and economic concerns?
- Do you ensure that your programmes are sustainable and have longevity, by regularly seeking feedback, evaluating and modifying them to keep them relevant? (The CEC website has an impact evaluation toolkit: https://resources.careersandenterprise.co.uk/impact-evaluation-toolkit.)

Investing the time to understand your stakeholders' pressures and priorities, learning about the challenges your young people may face when they transition from your institute and encouraging all staff to be able to see this bigger picture and the school's part in helping to prepare the students will help your programmes to be relevant and have longevity. You may need to adapt your chosen framework so that it is responsive to the needs and priorities of your stakeholders, therefore contributing to local economic growth and inclusive sustainability developments.

Labour market information (LMI) is an important topic in the English careers education system, as it features in the Gatsby Benchmarks, a framework used in schools and colleges for good careers education and guidance. Knowing what LMI is, how to find relevant LMI and how to use it are important for young people, their parents and teachers. Plenty of resources can be found on the Careers and Enterprise Company's website and many regional career hub websites, too. Key things to remember when you are integrating LMI into your SDE and sustainable career guidance programmes are:

- What are the dominant sectors in your locality, and how are they addressing decarbonisation and the move to net zero?
- Ensure opportunity to learn about and discuss entry-level jobs for all abilities, training and education opportunities. What 'green job' categories are these jobs in, and how would young people work this out (see chapter 4)?
- Be open about the mismatch between subjects studied at university and the job opportunities available. There is no reason for them not to study their favourite subject at degree level, but encourage exploration to help young people understand how their skills and experiences are transferrable.
- Arguably, all types of jobs and careers impact society and the planet, so create opportunities for young people to explore the positive, or negative, effects of their ideal career.

Every school and college will be at a different stage of incorporating SDE and sustainable career guidance into their day-to-day learning. Perhaps your institute is yet to embrace these practices; however, the fact that you are reading this book means that you're ready to take the next steps in creating a sustainable careers education programme that embraces sustainability. Where to start? A well-thought-out strategy can lead to a sustainable programme. Adapting the key points from the British Education Research Association's 'Manifesto for Education for Environmental Sustainability' could be useful to help you develop a SDE and sustainable careers education strategy.[6] Key points include:

- A coordinated review of secondary school curricula involving teachers and students.
- The environment should be part of all subjects and school practices.
- Sustainability coordinators to lead a school to a greener approach.
- A focus on the environment both outside and inside the classroom.
- Continuing professional development for teachers of all subjects.
- Externally accredited awards for students and teachers.[6]

Changing the way an organisation does something, such as delivering SDE and sustainable careers education, is a big task and will involve planning, and a Theory of Change may be a useful tool.[7] Very briefly, this involves the following:

- Identify the goals and intended outcomes of your programme.
- Map backwards to where you are now, the activities you already do and identify any changes that will be required to meet the goals.
- Draw connections between where you are now and where you want to get to.
- Identify the assumptions, such as people involved, resources, barriers and enablers, rationale and context for the programme.
- Identify the interventions required to ensure the implementation and success of the programme.
- Create a realistic timeline for reaching the goals.

Things to think about

Start with the mission and values of the school – is a link to the environment, community and the planet implied? Could this be more explicit and clearly defined?

What are the main priorities of the school in the development plan? Do they align with a more just society? How can sustainability in career guidance help to deliver the priorities?

Is sustainability within the school's governance? Could a sustainability policy be developed that includes the curriculum and career guidance, and how the school building and environment are managed? (For more information about the Department for Education's Sustainability and Climate Change Strategy and Climate Action Plans, see the section at the end of this chapter.)

Student-centred

Put the young person and their needs at the heart of your sustainability strategy and SDE programme. Some issues to be aware of include:

- **Climate change and global problems are problems that some young people may find overwhelming.** We can help them to see that any career they choose can have a positive effect on making things a little better. Every job can contribute, from a travelling method to helping a company work more efficiently and reduce waste.

- **What is decent work?** Help young people to understand what fair and decent work is. Deciding if a job is good or bad is subjective, and a range of factors need to be considered, including pay, hours worked, work environment, continuous professional development and career progression. Inequalities of early experiences of work and precarious work can affect a young person's transition. Part-time work while in full-time education can be a valuable learning experience, but this may not be taken seriously by some, and working too many hours may negatively affect learning.[8] However, be aware of the role of social pressures, as some young people may need to work.

World of work example: The Greater Manchester Good Employment Charter

Working with the community, employers, charities and local academics, the charter is a voluntary scheme that aims to 'elevate employment standards in Greater Manchester' (www.gmgoodemploymentcharter.co.uk/).

How this is useful:

Create learning opportunities for students to explore the seven characteristics of good work (secure work, flexible work, engagement and voice, recruitment, people management, health and well-being and pay), and have a go at the good employment quiz: www.goodemploymentweek.co.uk/quiz.

- **Understand employers' (local, national and global) 'skills demand'** and look at this through a 'green lens' (see chapter 3 for how to do this). Our ageing population increases the 'skills demand' as experienced, skilled workers retire. Developments in technologies change the skills in demand as new ways of using machine learning, data and artificial intelligence emerge. How does this affect the young people you work with? Does the curriculum on offer *really* meet your students' needs? Do they have the opportunity to explore what skills are in demand, and how their curriculum and other activities can help them to develop some of the skills?

Things to think about

Could you develop a 'skills bootcamp' by collaborating with local businesses, delivering short courses focusing on the (technical) skills employers would like their new employees to have? If you are a school, you may consider partnering with a local college to co-deliver workshops involving equipment the college may have. In longer term, the skills boot camp could be offered to the wider community.

- **Find out what young people care about.** Candy Ho, from the Kwantlen Polytechnic University, Canada, asks her students three questions:

    1. What is the world I want to live in?
    2. What do I see are the global problems or opportunities that need my attention?
    3. What are my talents and experiences that may help address these problems and in turn improve the condition of our world? (Adapted from NICEC presentation, 3 July 2024)[9]

Giving the time for these discussions can enable young people to leverage their skills, interests and talents towards a SDG. For example, if they have good media skills they can use them to share information about a charity event and students interested in law studies can find out about clean water legislation. In education, we can use the SDGs to explore career options and career purposes, but remember, not everyone wants to set the world on fire. Some people just want a job or career that gives them a comfortable life, and this is OK.

Interesting fact

In her book *Change Your Story* (2023, Wisdom Publishing), Carolyn Parry introduces each SDG and a variety of jobs related to addressing the aim of each goal. This could be a starting point for young people to research job opportunities available. However, if sustainability is a driver for an individual's career, help them to think critically about an organisation they want to work for or a job they want to do. Is the job description clear about how the work contributes to sustainability? Is the company's website misleading about its sustainability credentials (sometimes referred to as 'greenwashing')? How can we check?

Chapter 9: Sustainability and Career Education

Types of activity

If SDE is to be at the heart of your school/college, learning about the planet, climate change and sustainable development should come before detailed career education learning. Plan a range of activities that occur throughout the curriculum and a student's time at school/college. Think about the value of each and how it adds to a progressive SDE programme (see Table 9.2 for more information).

Table 9.2. Overview of a suggested progressive and sustainable SDE programme

Age	Outline of activities	Overarching purpose (adapted from Transformational Change models[7])
11-14	• Subject learning – (e.g. energy sources, climate change, biodiversity, water and waste). • Reduce, reuse and recycle (home, school and in the local community). • Social justice and local charities supporting the community (e.g. food banks, young carers). • Write a letter to future generations about what you plan to do to make the world a better place. (Idea adapted from the Wales Future Generations commission.)	Contemplation: Thinking about my place in the world.
14-16	• Subject learning. • What actions are sectors linked to a specific subject taking? • What is the circular economy? • Explore the UN Sustainable Development Goals (e.g. https://myfuture.edu.au/assist-others/sustainable-development-goals). • Exploring local further and higher education courses that focus on sustainability. • How will I make a difference? How could my career have an impact on the world? Which SDG resonates with me? Why?	Preparation: Understanding global problems.
16-18	• Subject learning. • Investigating the circular economy in their region. • Produce your 'Mission Statement' (see text box in this chapter) (adapted from the work of Candy Ho[9]). • Individual research, e.g. Extended Project Qualification.	Action: Imagining a future where my career and actions have a positive effect on society and the environment.

Below is a list of opportunities within school life that you may already be using:

- Within subjects (not just STEM and geography!);
- Within PSHE, or Health and Well-being curriculum time;
- Assemblies;
- Extracurricular;

- Trips and visits (including to local colleges and universities to learn about SDE courses and how the organisations address sustainability);
- External speakers/visitors (including alumni);
- Themed days/weeks (e.g. National Careers Week, British Science Week, Green Careers Week).

Do you have opportunities for local employers to visit the school/college? When employers speak to your students, could you 'prep' them to be able to share their carbon reduction strategies or allow your students to 'interview' visitors about their 'green' skills? It is mutually beneficial for employers to do this, as this helps to get young people into the labour market with the desired skills and as a school, you can help your students understand more about the local labour market and changes associated with the move to net zero.

More information about: Experiences of the workplace

Your current career programme probably has opportunities for some form of work experience. Experiences of the workplace are important at all stages of education, from visits to local companies, work shadowing days, formal work experience and professional internships. Enrich this by structuring the experience so that young people learn about:

- the business world and how the company works sustainably;
- expanding their network can lead to opportunities, such as extended work placements or summer jobs;
- experiential learning (tell, show, work shadow) to learn about how people experience *decent work* (see above for more information).

See case study 1 about Balfour Beatty in chapter 6 to find out how this company addresses sustainability.

How sustainable are your activities and programme? What do you need to put in place for the activity to occur regularly (e.g. added to the school diary and subject specifications)? Does one person or department have the responsibility? Is there succession planning to account for a turnover of staff? For a quick way to review an activity, use Figure 9.1. Ensure the students' preparation for the event is planned *and delivered*. Make it a meaningful event for a young person by having follow-up time that includes structured reflection and planning their next steps. You can think of this as the 'so what?'. (Remember, also do this for the 'one-off' events.)

Chapter 9: Sustainability and Career Education

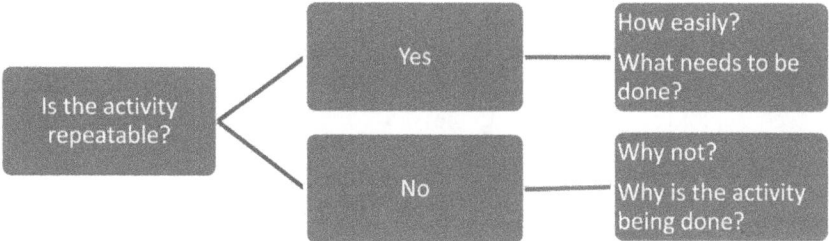

Figure 9.1. Planning for a sustainable careers education programme

How do you know if your programme is successful? How will you evaluate each activity and the overall programme? Steps to consider for a meaningful evaluation include:

- **Gather feedback** from participants, facilitators, visitors and staff overseeing (as soon as possible after the activity).
- **Interpret** the feedback (positive and negative, what patterns are there?).
- **Share** insights (with staff, facilitators and possible participants).
- **Act on** the insights, make arrangements to ensure the positive insights remain and modify the activity/programme to address any negative insights.

Consider how the activity supports subject learning and the wider curriculum. Table 9.3 gives an overview of the things you should consider for each activity, and Table 9.4 offers suggestions for specific subject areas. The mini case study about the WWF-UK Sustainable Futures programme explores how the charity developed resources for schools and evaluated the impact. Whether

Table 9.3. Things to consider when planning activities

What?	Type of activity? (e.g. assembly, workshop)
Who?	Year group? Class? Group characteristic? (e.g. gender, free school meals)
Where?	Within a specific subject? In form-time/cooperative learning/PSHE? Extracurricular?
When?	In lessons? Themed day/week? Lunchtime/after school?
Why?	What does the learning support? How are the students prepared?
How?	Which staff will deliver and how are they prepared? External visitors? (e.g. employers, alumni, training providers) How are the students prepared? Student-led?
So what?	What is the follow-up? How will reflection take place? How does this activity link to future activities?

you use this organisation's materials or not, there are lessons learned that can be applied to integrating any activity into a school's SDE and careers education programme. In the references section of the book, you will find more suggestions for resources and activities that can be used across the curriculum.

For evaluation resources visit the Careers and Enterprise Company website: https://resources.careersandenterprise.co.uk/resources/evaluation-guide-careers-activities-and-programmes.

Table 9.4. Suggested sustainable development education activities for curriculum areas

Subject	Suggested activities
Maths	Use sustainable development issues for data collection and data handling activities, for example, gathering information about recycling. Analyse the data for the progress of the 17 UN SDGs (infographics and progress data available for each goal: https://sdgs.un.org/goals).
English	Consider 'sustainability' in each set text (environmental, social and economic), for example, the movement of Birnam Wood in Macbeth and the economic and social differences between the characters in *An Inspector Calls*. Use sustainable development issues as a vehicle to develop writing techniques, for example, poetry or persuasive writing.
Science	Explicit throughout the curriculum, but be creative, for example: • How 'green' is your lab (see chapter 7)? • Financial implications of 'green' technologies and a socially just and fair transition.
Technology	Implicit throughout the curriculum, create opportunities to explore, for example: • How 'green' is your workshop? • How sustainable are the materials you use (from raw materials, production, lifespan and recycling)?
Modern foreign languages	The UN SDGs are global. Explore the work being done in countries that speak the language your students are learning. Use sustainable development issues (environmental, economic and social) as the vehicle for developing academic skills in the language studied.
Geography	Explore local authority road improvement and town planning schemes, use maps and consider the different roles involved, for example, to complete the Environmental Impact Assessment. Set a local 'town planning' challenge (see Swift Street activity in the Further Resources section below).
History	There are concerns about how AI and other technological advancements will affect the workforce. Explore how technological developments across the ages, for example, the printing press and steam-powered looms, have affected society. What are the lessons learnt, and how can the future workforce use this to prepare?
Performing arts	Spoken word, dance and music are all powerful ways to explore issues and get a message to the wider community. How are the issues your students are learning in other subjects affecting them? How can performing arts be used to help young people express themselves?
PE	Being physically active is important; how does your school environment encourage this? Are there areas in the community that could be improved to make exercising safer?

Subject-specific activities

Subject teachers will know best how to weave sustainable development into their programmes of study, but if starting ideas are needed for inspiration, share Table 9.4 with your teaching colleagues.

MINI CASE STUDY: WWF-UK SUSTAINABLE FUTURES PROGRAMME

This is an example of a charity's education resource, WWF-UK Sustainable Futures, developed in partnership with Villiers Park Educational Trust and Founders4Schools.

The Sustainable Futures programme could be used to embed learning about sustainable careers into a school/college's existing programme or as a stand-alone resource. There are three fully resourced sections:

1. Module 1: What is sustainability (including values, SDGs and systems thinking)?
2. Module 2: Sustainable business (including doughnut economics and greenwashing).
3. Module 3: Sustainable me (including careers, skills and a sustainable career).

There is also a taster session for students and CPD videos to support teachers delivering the programme.

In 2024, a comprehensive evaluation was conducted by the International Centre for Guidance Studies (iCeGS) at the University of Derby. Students, educators and employer stakeholders were involved in the process, and information was gathered via surveys, focus groups and interviews. Key findings showed that students increased their understanding of sustainability and how careers are linked to sustainability. The main recommendation is for the programme to enhance the strategic engagement with business, strengthening collaboration between educators and employers.

- www.wwf.org.uk/get-involved/schools/sustainable-futures
- https://repository.derby.ac.uk/download/219a544755342c545e7eeb97915508ef1be7e525a51ac9f455e238664ee46af5/2724495/UoD_iCeGS_Annual%20Review%202024.pdf

More information about: Writing a 'mission statement'

Plan an activity for students to write their mission statement with rationale:

- What are your values and/or skills (see *STEM Careers* (2nd edition) for further guidance on exploring skills and values)?
- Who you are creating your mission statement for (yourself, a college/university application, a future employer)?
- The expected outcome/goal (e.g. making an event happen, getting onto a course, securing a job).
- The SDG you are aiming to progress (see activities in age 14–16 section of Table 9.2).

Perhaps you can have a go at writing your mission statement before asking students to write theirs. (Adapted from the work of Candy Ho.[9])

World of work example: Green Careers Hub

Hosted by the Institute of Sustainability and Environmental Professionals (ISEP), formally known as the Institute of Environmental Management and Assessment (IEMA), the Green Careers Hub website (www.greencareershub.com) provides information about green skills, green jobs and the green economy. There are career stories, job profiles, videos from partnership organisations (involved in engineering, conservation, housing and research) as well as live job opportunities.

How this is useful:

Careers advisers can use this website during personal guidance meetings and small group work. Form teachers can use this website with their tutor groups and during themed activities. Teachers can use job profiles and case studies when linking their subjects to the world of work.

Interesting fact

Nesta is the UK's innovation agency for social good, whose mission is to help all young people have a fairer start in life, to narrow health inequalities in the UK and to help us all to have a sustainable future.

They have developed a range of evidence-based toolkits to help organisations engage with evidence, frame activities and progress their goals. Explore Nesta's resources that could be adapted for use with colleagues and students: www.nesta.org.uk/toolkit/.

Chapter 9: Sustainability and Career Education

More information about: The Department for Education's Sustainability and Climate Change Strategy

The UK is committed to be net zero by 2050, and schools and colleges have a part to play in this. In 2022 the DfE launched its sustainability and climate change strategy that is divided into five areas:

1. Climate education;
2. Green skills and careers;
3. Education estate and digital infrastructure;
4. Operations and supply chain;
5. International.

The vision is that the UK will have a world leading education sector in sustainability and climate change by 2030, with **all education settings in England having a Climate Action Plan in place by the end of 2025**. This should include plans for curricular and extracurricular activity, procurement, adaptation and resilience of buildings and site and decarbonisation.

For more information

- Read about the DfE's strategy: www.gov.uk/government/publications/sustainability-and-climate-change-strategy/9317e6ed-6c80-4eb9-be6d-3fcb1f232f3a.
- To find support with setting up your school's Climate Action Plan, visit: www.sustainabilitysupportforeducation.org.uk.
- For developments in coordinating what climate education is, visit: www.reading.ac.uk/planet/climate-education/climate-education-plan.
- In chapter 9 find out about the work that can be done in schools to address sustainability, in governance, leadership and the curriculum.

MINI CASE STUDY: CLIMATE ACTION PLANS AND SUFFOLK EDUCATION

All schools in England are required to have a Climate Action Plan by the end of 2025. In partnership, all Suffolk councils are supporting schools with this through their Sustainable Schools Network. Rebecca Elston-Haynes, Suffolk's Schools Sustainability Lead, says, 'Schools should have a sustainability lead and their Climate Action Plan should have sections on decarbonisation, biodiversity, green climate education and green careers, and adaptation and resilience.' Rebecca added, 'The Department for Education (DfE) clarified what should be in a Climate Action Plan . . . [however] schools aren't very aware of this guidance.'

Rebecca describes that many organisations have been working in this space for a long time, and the offers of help can be confusing for schools. However, the DfE funds three main programmes:

1. To help schools support and improve the biodiversity within their grounds, the organisation **National Education Nature Park** offers a free programme that provides guidance and resources for teachers to embed climate and nature learning into the school's setting. Rebecca explains, 'If you take all the green areas or the potential green areas [in school grounds], then you have quite a large area. We want to try and develop the biodiversity. So they've developed digital tools . . . one is to map the boundaries of your site . . . and create a vision for your school and what that would look like' (www.educationnaturepark.org.uk).
2. **Climate Ambassadors** work with nurseries, schools and colleges in England. 'This is a bank of people that schools can call upon to support them right in their climate action plans or delivering things like climate education', says Rebecca (https://climateambassadors.org.uk/).
3. An online resource from the DfE offering **Sustainability Support for Education** can be tailored to a school's setting and priorities, helping them to plan their sustainability journey. Rebecca sees this 'as a one stop shop for like all your sustainability resources'. This is in development and new resources are regularly added (www.sustainabilitysupportforeducation.org.uk).

Rebecca describes an additional campaign that schools can join. Let's Go Zero unites schools across the UK, supporting them to cut carbon emissions to zero by 2030. This is funded by Ashden, an organisation with a mission to 'accelerate transformative climate solutions and build a more just world' (https://ashden.org/). The funding is complex and not all of the free services are available to each home nation; for example, their climate action advisers can only help schools in England with climate action planning. For more information, visit Let's Go Zero: https://letsgozero.org/.

Each council in England has its own approach to running its climate emergency plans, and Rebecca advises schools to find out what specific support is available for education from their local authority. This may be through careers services, PSHE support or specialist sustainability leads.

Rebecca's role involves partnership working with the national organisations offering sustainability in schools programmes and working with Suffolk secondary schools that want support with their sustainability journey, developing a teacher network for learning and sharing. Carbon literacy training has been made available and other workshops are planned. The team Rebecca is part of developed the Green Suffolk Youth Climate Conference in 2023. Attendance grew to 250 young people in 2024, and the team has exciting plans for the 2025 conference.

There are challenges and barriers in getting schools to become more sustainable and develop the education for sustainable development programmes. Rebecca concludes that behaviour change is key to schools making progress with producing their Climate Action Plans. The support from senior leaders is required, as is adequate funding to assist schools in their learning and development.

Find out more about the work taking place in Suffolk: www.greensuffolk.org/suffolk-schools-are-taking-action-against-climate-change/.

Sustainability Governor

'Creating a role for a Sustainability Governor supports the school in meeting the ambitions of the DfE's Sustainability and Climate Strategy. Through learning walks, attending events and meetings with leaders and operations staff, a Sustainability Governor can champion the hard work and passion of school staff and pupils. The role provides a voice for climate and nature as part of a school's governance and leadership structure in a sector that juggles competing curriculum pressures, school development priorities and budgets.

'I am proud of the connections created between the school and local organisations for the launch of its first Green Careers Fair in 2022 and linking to local authority expertise for its first Sustainability drop-down day in 2025. However, I am most proud of the staff and pupils who are committed through their everyday actions, and in particular the leadership, enthusiasm and resilience shown by everyone in the school's Gardening and Sustainability club.

'We have a duty of care for our young people's futures. Whether that's providing a greener environment for them or supporting their climate literacy, understanding of sustainability skills and awareness of green jobs, there is much to do. A Sustainability Governor can be a critical friend, bringing support, community links and knowledge that can help schools rise to the challenge presented.'

Karen Cannard, Sustainability Governor at Sybil Andrews Academy

For more information about appointing a Sustainability Governor, visit: www.sustainabilitysupportforeducation.org.uk/indicator/appoint-governor.

School Business Leadership

The Institute of School Business Leadership (ISBL) has designed sustainability standards 'to help ensure climate action and work to improve biodiversity are not treated as secondary considerations but as cornerstones to running a successful school or trust' (www.isbl.org.uk). These are an addendum to the Professional Standards Framework and relate to the following areas: operational leadership, finance, procurement, human resources, estate management and marketing and communications.

Conclusion

Sustainable development education (SDE) involves teaching students *about* sustainable development, for example, as done in science and geography, and teaching *for* sustainable development so that young people develop the values and skills to become globally aware citizens who can contribute to a just and sustainable world.

This chapter discusses how to develop a strategy and programme for SDE and sustainable career education that serves the needs of the students. If we can help young people improve their knowledge and understanding of the environment, the effect human activities have upon it, the net zero economy and the move towards reducing carbon emissions, they can make more informed choices at transition times.

Ideally, developing a SDE programme should be led 'top-down' with the strategic leadership team developing strategies, policies and improvements that refer to sustainability in the day-to-day operations and curriculum. This should also be 'student-led', with young people able to champion the causes they are passionate about, interrogate procedures and contribute to developments. Read the case study from Bedford Academy to find out how they are embedding sustainability through the heart of the school, overcoming challenges and making the world a better place.

Your SDE programme should itself be sustainable, limiting the 'one-offs' and planning activities that are deliverable each academic year. There are frameworks, such as the UN Sustainable Development Goals, the CDI's framework and Hooley and Dimsits' five dimensions for environmentally sustainable career guidance, that you can use to guide your programme to ensure that it is relevant, meeting the needs of the students, staff and wider community.

Chapter 10 will help you to pull together the key messages from this book and begin planning your next steps.

CASE STUDY 4 – BEDFORD ACADEMY

This is a study of a school, Bedford Academy, which has sustainability at the heart of how it operates, both in terms of the day-to-day running of the school and incorporating sustainability into the curriculum (subject, careers education and extracurricular).

By learning how this school is approaching sustainability, teachers and careers professionals can plan how they will develop their next steps for a sustainable school and a successful SDE programme.

Introduction to the school

Bedford Academy, part of the HEART Academies Trust in Bedfordshire, is a community-minded school that puts its students at the centre of everything it does. Head teacher, Chris Deller, explains that 'the school's vision, values and ethos are at the centre of all our efforts to bring about generational change to the local community. We strive to ensure that the quality of the educational experience that students receive is an ever-improving picture, and that every individual embarks on a pathway that matches their long-term aspirations.'

In 2023, the Trust set up a Schools Sustainability Network, affiliated to the UK Schools Sustainability Network (UKSSN), to help primary and secondary schools become greener and Bedford Academy has been central to this. Driven by Paul Edmond, HEART Academies Trust's Chief Finance and Sustainability Officer, the Trust has pledged to become carbon zero by 2030, commissioning experts to help schools reduce their carbon footprint by investing in renewable energy and energy-efficient technologies.

Bedford Academy relies on the UN SDGs to guide in the 17 areas it covers, adding the icons to the front page of Trust-wide action plans, serving as a timely reminder of what they are collaborating to achieve. The HEART Academies Trust is responsible for the provision of data to the school, using Planet Mark to obtain full carbon footprint reports that can be used to measure the impact of the sustainability initiatives. Regular updates are provided via briefings and emails, helping to keep the profile of sustainability high.

Bedford Academy has a strong careers programme and in 2019 achieved 'Best School or College of the Year' at the Careers Excellence Awards, hosted by the Careers and Enterprise Company. This was followed by successfully gaining the Quality in Careers Standard in 2022.

Operational approach to sustainability

Bedford Academy prides itself on being at the heart of the community and, therefore, has a responsibility to the surrounding community – as well as staff and students – to demonstrate its commitment to sustainability. The school works hard to incorporate the HEART Trust Climate Action Plan into everyday sustainability without compromising the standard of education.

The school has invested in its estate and has upgraded its Building Energy Management System (BEMS) and has recently opened a new two-story carbon neutral building. Students were engaged with the building project from the start, learning about the energy saving design and about careers in sustainable construction. The school strives to reduce its energy baseload, which is the fastest way to reduce energy costs and its carbon footprint. Methods the school employs to be more sustainable include:

- commissioning Green Net Zero to carry out building energy surveys;
- using Energy Sparks to track and report energy use;
- installing digital water metre readers to track usage and identify leaks;
- the finance team are working with Value Match to support procurement and partnerships with suppliers that actively promote sustainability and social value;
- working with the Peterborough Environment City Trust (PECT) to identify opportunities to improve biodiversity in the school grounds;
- employing paper purchase reduction techniques to monitor the printing of each member of staff and students with users sent an alert if a certain threshold is reached;
- encouraging staff to switch off water chillers, smart boards and projectors, hot drink urns and extraction fans when not required;
- investing in window film to reduce heat loss.

The food reflects a variety of tastes and cultures. The menu has been designed so that there is a mixture of vegetarian and vegan dishes options. The school is proud to confirm its commitment to sustainability by reducing the menu's content of red meat to one main dish every three weeks. Where applicable, all chicken, turkey, beef and lamb are Halal and food waste turned into compost for grounds.

The school has four electric vehicle (EV) chargers, and employees can use the chargers for free. As 20% of HEART Trust's carbon footprint relates to employees commuting, the EV chargers have a dual purpose, to improve air quality in the vicinity of our school and to reduce the Trust carbon footprint. The school also plans to work with Bedford Borough Council to monitor air quality in the local vicinity.

Paul Edmond outlines future operational plans that Bedford Academy has:

- Investing in more solar photovoltaic panels;
- Assessing new digital technology to track and manage plant and equipment efficiency;
- Switch to purchasing 100% renewable electricity;
- Investment in energy-efficient ICT (e.g. front-of-class screens);
- Investment in tree planting.

Curriculum approach to sustainability

Sustainability has become part of the daily life at Bedford Academy, and the school has a 'Careers Charter' that is shared with students. A careers learning logo is used by teachers to highlight when career learning is taking place in the classroom.

During their Green Careers Week 2024, the school invited Planet Mark to deliver workshops to students. Year 9 learnt about marketing and sustainability, including potentially contentious issues such as branding, labour conditions and impact on the environment. A range of visitors throughout the week enabled students to learn about a range of careers linked to sustainability. Organisations that attended the Green Careers Week included a construction company, a local Wildlife Trust group and a geoscience technology company. An alumnus who is undertaking an apprenticeship in Sustainability and Governance with a real estate firm also visited the students. These encounters with employers gave the students opportunities to learn more about sustainability in the workplace and across different sectors.

Students

Students are actively engaged in driving the changes and improvements the school is making to become more sustainable.

There is an **Eco Council** that all students in years 7 to 13 are welcome to join. The group has around 18 members, primarily years 7, 8 and 9 with one Year 12 student who is the sustainability prefect. Meetings are usually held every other week, with discussions focusing on topics such as waste, diet, transport and politics. Activities the Eco Council have undertaken include visits to nature parks and climate summits, debates alongside the school's debate club, nature photography walks and sustainability projects. The group also took part in the Green Schools Project's 26-week course (www.greenschoolsproject.org.uk). The work of the Eco Council is fed back to all students in school via form time or in assemblies. Climate emails are sent out every term reminding staff and students about paper usage, heating usage and to switch off power to avoid standby, and weekly sustainability emails are sent to help people catch up with green affairs in and around the world.

One other initiative is in partnership with Future Foundations, regularly hosting CANTeam afterschool dining events. This is co-designed with young people encouraging students and their families to enjoy a meal together, promoting inclusion within the community. The CANTeam also promote sustainable food and eating as part of their community events.

For more information visit: www.future-foundations.co.uk/myexperience-with-canteam/.

Other community activities that the students can be involved in include:

- The Bedford Repair Cafe that the school hosts. Volunteers repairing anything, such as TVs, bikes and clothes, reducing the amount of stuff sent to landfill.
- Preloved and Baby Bank. The school has hosted this since 2023 of items for reusing/swapping, such as buggies, moses baskets and breast pumps.
- The Bedford Re-track project, helping vulnerable members of the community.
- Students and staff regularly visit food banks to encourage widespread acknowledgement of food waste and surplus.
- The school works in partnership with Olio, a sharing app, to distribute food to the local community and help minimise food waste.

Careers perspective

Nicola Simons, Careers Adviser and Work Experience Coordinator, shares her golden nuggets and plans for careers and sustainability:

- Work with Planet Mark to deliver a year-group-wide initiative for interactive and sustainability-focused workshops during Green Careers Week.

- Continuously identifying opportunities for expanding the school's employer network, particularly those who work in Environment, Sustainability and Governance (ESG).
- Work with the Sixth Form Sustainability Lead on projects and opportunities to showcase Green Careers for older students in the school.
- Encourage engagement of Bedford Academy's younger students with sustainability careers work.
- Continue to review and reach out to suppliers, supported by the school's finance team, to support the school's plans for a year-round programme of green events.
- Endorse green career options at as many school events as possible and ensure there is a careers representative present to promote green career opportunities.

Challenges

As with any organisational change, there are challenges that the school must face. Paul describes three main areas:

- **Curriculum** – adapting the curriculum in a way that supports sustainability education is difficult. Research on how to do this effectively is limited and so we are working with the CAPE Alliance of schools and Trusts to explore this (www.capealliance.org.uk). We are also waiting for the outcome of the curriculum review.
- **Knowledge** – we need to increase training and understanding of climate change and [its] links to schools and education.
- **Funding** – we don't have the money for some of the work we would like to do, for example, replacing gas boilers with air-source heat pumps.

Future plans

The school has exciting plans for future developments that include:

1. Expand the work of the Eco Council;
2. Exploring links with businesses in relation to careers;
3. Include eco-education in more subject curricula;
4. Invest in a poly-tunnel to expand horticulture provision;
5. Signing up to the National Education Nature Park.

The long-term goals for Bedford Academy are:

- Become a net zero school;
- Increase the teaching of sustainability and climate change in the curriculum;
- Improved use of school grounds to benefit biodiversity;
- Partnerships with the private sector to support sustainability.

Advice for schools

Paul offers the following advice for schools that want to become more sustainable and support sustainability:

- Develop a **Climate Action Plan** (CAP) in consultation with experts. A CAP needs to be tailored to the context of the school and community.
- Invest in **Climate Leadership** – make sure this is a clearly defined role with resources to support effective action.
- Build a **sustainability group** that includes people from across different areas of the school (governance, operational, academic) with a passion for nature and the skills to make a difference.
- Invest in **training/CPD** – carbon literacy is critical. Conferences and training are available and accessible.
- Invest in **capturing data** – energy, water, waste, biodiversity, carbon footprint – data is critical to measure progress and set targets.
- Work in **partnership** – there are organisations that can support you: UKSSN, Let's Go Zero, Climate Ambassadors, National Education Nature Park, Value Match, plus specialists with specific knowledge, e.g. curriculum, catering, careers.
- Each Trust and school will approach this differently, but if you can start to do lots of little things, they will all add up.

To find out more about Bedford Academy, visit: www.bedfordacademy.co.uk/.

Selection of resources for schools and colleges

Whole school approach

- **National Education Nature Park and Climate Awards:** Backed by the DfE and linked with national environmental charities. Sign up for free programmes, case studies and other resources to help you have a whole school approach to using nature to benefit students, staff and the school environment (www.educationnaturepark.org.uk).

- **Eco Schools:** (Part of Keep Britain Tidy) (www.eco-schools.org.uk).
- **Green Schools Project:** 'Help your school get serious about sustainability' (www.greenschoolsproject.org.uk).
- **UK Schools Sustainability Network:** A community of over 7,000 educators empowering students to take climate action (linked to Green School Project) (https://www.transform-our-world.org/home).
- **Change Makers:** Provide courses for educators and young people (www.changemakers.com/en).
- **EUK Education: Climate – Schools Programme** Gives you the resources, knowledge and confidence to address the climate crisis with your students (https://eukeducation.org.uk/our-programmes/climate-schools-programme).
- **UNESCO** Greening every curriculum: Guidance to teach and learn for climate action (www.unesco.org/en/education-sustainable-development/greening-future/curriculum).
- **Students Organising for Sustainability (SOS-UK):** A student-led education charity focusing on sustainability (https://www.sos-uk.org/).
- **The Sustainability Exchange:** Resources for sustainability in post-16 education (www.sustainabilityexchange.ac.uk).
- **British Ecological Society Education:** Schools' outreach project to green their environment (www.britishecologicalsociety.org/learning-and-resources/connecting-schools-to-nature/).
- **Green Careers week:** (https://greencareersweek.com/).
- **National Career's week Green Buzz Quiz:** Linked to green skills, career advice and career suggestions (https://nationalcareersweek.com/green-buzz).
- **National Energy Action:** A range of resources for all age groups (primary and secondary) promoting the efficient use of energy and achieving affordable warmth at home (www.nea.org.uk/training/education-resources/).
- **Keep Scotland Beautiful:** This organisation has a wealth of resources based around the Climate Action Schools framework (www.keepscotlandbeautiful.org/climate-action-schools/).
- **Keep Wales Tidy and Keep Northern Ireland Tidy:** These organisations collaborate with the global Eco-Schools programme providing a seven-step framework for schools to embed education for sustainable development, develop students' skills and 'drive positive environmental change' (keepwalestidy.cymru/eco-schools/ and www.eco-schoolsni.org).

Linked to SDGs

- **My Future**: An Australian careers website for students, teachers and parents. Includes worksheets, card sorts and teacher guides (https://myfuture.edu.au/assist-others/sustainable-development-goals).

Linked to STEM subjects

- **Science** (Scotland): A one-hour session for 16–18-year-olds exploring renewable energy careers, including non-STEM roles (https://nationalschoolspartnership.com/initiatives/field-power-up-career-exploration-challenge/).
- **Destination STEM:** Designated site for young people from STEM Learning (https://www.destinationstem.org.uk/).
- **Technology:** Go Construct has a range of resources linked to the built environment, electricity distribution and sustainability (www.goconstruct.org/educational-resources/resources-for-teachers/key-stage-4/).
- **Engineering:** Biannual competition of civil engineering challenges, using computer games to develop skills such as teamwork, critical thinking, communication and problem-solving to build a better world (www.ice.org.uk/your-career/education-resources/teaching-resources/ice-cityzen-competitions).
- **Maths:** A range of resources that use climate and sustainability as a context for teaching maths (https://mei.org.uk/about-mei/what-we-do/current-projects-and-programmes/climate-change-and-sustainability-as-context-in-maths-teaching/).
- **Oak National Academy** has a range of resources for teaching sustainability linked to science, geography and design and technology (www.thenational.academy/teachers/search?term=sustainability).
- **See it Be it:** One-hour lesson resources based on a job role (mainly STEM) presentation, video and PDF notes included (https://seeitbeit.org.uk/resources-for-schools).

Chapter 10
Wrapping up

> Use the key messages from this book to plan your next steps.

Introduction

The pun in this chapter title is intended. For over 20 years, the global organisation WRAP has been on a mission 'to embed circular living in every boardroom and every home'.[1] With circular living, resources are used more carefully, benefitting society across the globe and protecting nature, now and for future generations. WRAP works with governments, companies and individuals across the world. As a parent, teacher or career professional, you may think your sphere of influence won't have a significant impact; however, young people have been disrupting the norm and pushing for change for generations. We just need to add oxygen to their flame.

We all have a part to play in improving the environment so that nature, society and the economy can flourish for the benefit of everyone. Whether you are a subject teacher or a careers professional, adults supporting young people are in a key position to influence, encourage and support the next generation to see this, directly or indirectly, as part of their career.

Sustainability and careers are huge topics, and presenting these ideas in a format that will be useful has felt a bit like herding cats! The main themes throughout this book are: sustainability and careers, having a sustainable career and sustainable development education.

1. **Sustainability and careers:** The types of 'green jobs' and skills required for sectors to reduce their greenhouse gas emissions (for the UK to reach net zero by 2050) and encourage nature restoration (mainly chapters 4, 5, 6 and 7).

2. **A sustainable career:** Preparing young people for a sustainable career that gives them decent work and prepares them for lifelong learning that doesn't negatively affect their mental health (mainly chapters 3 and 9).

3. **Sustainable development education (SDE):** Teaching *about* and teaching *for* sustainable development (mainly chapters 2, 8 and 9).

These themes are linked by a 'golden thread' of the UN Sustainable Development Goals (SDGs). (See chapter 2 for more information.) The SDGs can be used to give you topics to discuss with young people and as a framework for planning school strategy and education programmes. Your students can use the goals to explore what is important to them in their lives, the world they live in and how they might have a positive impact on their community and the environment.

In this chapter, we will review why this is important and how we can prepare our young people for meaningful, decent work. Hopefully, you feel 'fired up' and ready to push your ideas forward, therefore strategies to help you plan your next steps will also be discussed.

Why is the topic of sustainability important?

In 2009, researchers from the Stockholm Resilience Centre proposed a framework of nine planetary boundaries, based on earth science, human activity and the resilience of the Earth's systems to overcome our excesses. Their research showed that at the time, we had transgressed at least three of the nine boundaries. Ongoing research has found that by 2023 we had crossed six of the nine boundaries.[2] (See Table 10.1 for more information.)

All is not lost. Remember how we reduced our use of chlorofluorocarbons (CFCs) in aerosol cans and refrigerators in the 1980s and 1990s? This is a great example of how we reversed the negative effect humans had on one of the planetary boundaries (stratospheric ozone depletion). With similar willpower from individuals, communities and, importantly, governments, we can reverse the damage being done to our planet. The UK and home nations governments have developed policies to address climate change, by reducing our greenhouse gas emissions, focusing on nature restoration and improving biodiversity.

Why do young people need to learn about having a sustainable career?

Sustainability and careers are complex concepts that involve many disciplines, all sectors, organisations and individuals. This is not just

Chapter 10: Wrapping Up

Table 10.1. The nine planetary boundaries[2]

Planetary boundary	Explanation	Status
Climate change	Temperature increases due to trapped greenhouse gases.	Human activity is exceeding the Earth's ability to correct the system.
Novel entities	Synthetic materials such as plastics, substances that have been released due to human activity, such as radioactive materials and heavy metals, and species modified by human intervention, such as genetically modified organisms.	Human activity is exceeding the Earth's ability to correct the system.
Stratospheric ozone depletion	Protects living organisms on Earth from the harmful effects of ultraviolet radiation.	Within safe operating limits.
Atmospheric aerosol loading	Airborne particles from natural sources and human activity.	Within safe operating limits.
Ocean acidification	Carbon dioxide is naturally absorbed into the oceans, making sea water more acidic.	Within safe operating limits.
Biogeochemical flows	Modifications of the phosphorus and nitrogen cycles.	Human activity is exceeding the Earth's ability to correct the system.
Freshwater change	The water cycles in rivers and lakes, as well as the moisture in soil.	Human activity is exceeding the Earth's ability to correct the system.
Land system change	Changes to the natural landscape due to urbanisation and deforestation affecting habitats.	Human activity is exceeding the Earth's ability to correct the system.
Biosphere integrity	The effect of biodiversity loss, species and genetic, on the global ecosystem.	Human activity is exceeding the Earth's ability to correct the system.

For more information about the nine planetary boundaries visit: www.stockholmresilience.org/research/planetary-boundaries.html

for students interested in science, technology, engineering and maths (STEM). Every job has a part to play as we progress to a net zero economy, and this can be seen in the descriptions for some job adverts. Encourage young people to be open-minded about their 'work experiences'; learning about business and sustainability strategies can be applied to any industry or sector.

Donald, Van der Heijden and Baruch (2024) introduce sustainable career ecosystem theory.[3] In today's world, learning is a lifelong journey and education and the workplace are intertwined. People will need to keep learning new skills, upskilling and probably switch careers through retraining. By understanding this early on, especially while still in school, young people can develop good habits that will help them throughout their working lives. Encouraging young people to see learning as an ongoing process helps them stay adaptable and ready for new opportunities, preparing them to make meaningful contributions to their workplaces and society as a whole.

Good mental health and well-being are associated with having a meaningful career, and poor transitions can affect this. Various studies have investigated the lifelong consequences for people based on their transition from education to work. Sabates, Harris and Staff (2011) showed that misaligned or uncertain career aspirations when at school can compromise educational and career goals, which in turn can affect employment stability and 'the construction of life paths'.[4] In their work, Mousteri, Daly and Delaney (2018) investigated data from a wider study of 50+ year-olds across Europe to show that periods of unemployment of 6 months or more earlier in life caused psychological scarring that reduced well-being.[5]

There are challenges

As discussed in chapter 8, there are tensions and potential conflicts within the topics of sustainability and careers, and their intersection makes this even more complex. Three considerations are:

- **Technological developments** – Sector priorities can change rapidly. How does a teacher or career professional keep up with this? Are there sector websites and social media channels that you can subscribe to?
- **Ethics** – People have the right to make choices, or not, about their careers. The CDI Code of Ethics can help you be impartial, as an individual may have greater concerns than the environment or may not want their career to focus on this.
- **Politics** – Education and training policies can change, and financial implications can affect your plans. How can you and your school/college mitigate this? What are your priorities?

Planning your next steps

How do you move forward, as a subject teacher, career leader, qualified career development professional or school leader? Start by reflecting on where you or your school are right now, perhaps using a reflection framework (see examples of questions in the text box). A SWOT analysis (see Tables 10.2 and 10.3) is a simple, powerful tool that you can use to evaluate your (or your school/college's) strengths, weaknesses, opportunities and threats related to your SDE or career education programme. By evaluating these areas, you can develop strategies to leverage your strengths, address weaknesses, capitalise on opportunities and mitigate threats. This can lead to more effective and sustainable career and SDE programmes.

Things to think about

- Does your school have a Climate Action Plan and a designated sustainability lead?
- What sustainability conversations are taking place, for example, in building and ground maintenance, procurement and catering?
- Are students already involved in sustainability projects, for example, in an Eco-club?
- How are curriculum areas teaching *about* sustainability, for example, science, geography and technology?
- How is the wider curriculum teaching *for* sustainability, for example, in form-time and personal, social, health and economic (PSHE) education?
- Are the SDGs used within school/college, and how are they used (e.g. in strategy or teaching)?

Table 10.2. Example of a SWOT analysis for an individual teacher or career professional

Strengths For example: • Already have an understanding of sustainability issues. • Have the capacity to review your practice. • Good understanding of the world of work and 'green jobs'.	Weaknesses For example: • Know very little about sustainability. • Do not understand elements of the sustainability agenda (net zero, nature restoration). • Lack of knowledge about sector developments and jobs.
Opportunities For example: • School/college are embracing sustainability. • Opportunity for individuals to have training.	Threats For example: • No support (time or financial) for individuals to access training.

Table 10.3. Example of a SWOT analysis for an educational programme (Microsoft Copilot was used to help with this.)

Strengths For example: • Well-developed curriculum and teaching materials. • Qualified and passionate teachers and practitioners. • Strong involvement from students, parents, employers and local organisations.	Weaknesses For example: • Insufficient funding or materials. • Lack of access to modern technology. • Gaps in student motivation, achievement and opportunities.
Opportunities For example: • Use of emerging technologies, such as online learning platforms, virtual reality and AI. • Collaboration with business, higher education and other local organisations. • Curriculum development of new subjects and new teaching methods.	Threats For example: • Reduction in funding and resources. • Policy changes and new regulations that might impact the programmes. • Competition with other initiatives that could attract staff attention, students' interest and resources.

Conclusion

Considering sustainability and how it is linked to an individual's career is complex, and it is hoped that this book provides a 'route through', helping you to understand global and national agendas, sector developments and the role of education.

The book is a practical resource. I hope you find the 'Interesting facts', 'World of Work' examples and 'Things to think about' informative, providing you with examples to share with young people in the classroom and guidance meetings.

The four main case studies and mini case studies give examples of how organisations and individuals are working sustainably and changing behaviours, endeavouring to balance resources and finances for the benefit of society and the environment. I am grateful to the individuals and companies that shared their stories so that we can learn and inform our practice.

Supporting young people to understand that the workplace is changing is exciting. Some jobs may not change much and new ones will appear, but the key message is that there will always be new skills to learn and new technology to embrace.

To finish, although the UN SDGs provide an internationally recognised framework, they can also be *your* starting point. Who wouldn't want a world with zero hunger, quality education, affordable and clean energy, reduced inequalities, improved biodiversity and decent work for all? What do the young people you support have to say about that?

Whether taking your first steps with understanding sustainable development and career or developing your practice, good luck!

References for each chapter

Chapter 1 – Setting the scene

1. Purvis, B., Mao, Y. & Robinson, D. (2019) Three pillars of sustainability: In search of conceptual origins. *Sustainability Science* 14, 681–695. https://doi.org/10.1007/s11625-018-0627-5 [Accessed 11 June 2024]
2. WWF (2019) Putting people at the heart of the green transition. https://www.wwf.org.uk/green-transition [Accessed 11 June 2024]
3. European Training Foundation (2022) Skills for green transition. https://www.etf.europa.eu/sites/default/files/2022-11/Edited%20green%20transition%20policy%20brief_EN.pdf?trk=public_post_comment-text [Accessed 11 June 2024]
4. The British Geological Survey: Discovering Geology – Climate change. https://www.bgs.ac.uk/discovering-geology/climate-change/how-does-the-greenhouse-effect-work/ [Accessed 24 June 2024]
5. UK Government (2023) https://www.gov.uk/guidance/climate-change-explained [Accessed 24 June 2024]
6. UK Government (2022) https://www.gov.uk/government/publications/net-zero-strategy
7. Hockey, J. A. (2024) When private meets public: Young people and political consumerism in the name of environmental activism. *Journal of Youth Studies*, 1–18. https://doi.org/10.1080/13676261.2024.2370275 [Accessed 16 July 2024]
8. United Nations: Sustainable Development Goals (2024) https://www.un.org/sustainabledevelopment/sustainable-development-goals/ [Accessed 24 June 2024]

For information about the home nation's net zero work, visit:

- Scotland https://www.netzeronation.scot/
- Northern Ireland https://www.daera-ni.gov.uk/articles/green-growth-strategy-northern-ireland-balancing-our-climate-environment-and-economy
- Wales https://www.gov.wales/net-zero-wales

Chapter 2 - The United Nations Sustainable Development Goals

1. United Nations Sustainable Development Goals (2024) https://sdgs.un.org/ [Accessed 25 June 2024]
2. UK Government (2019) www.gov.uk/government/publications/implementing-the-sustainable-development-goals/implementing-the-sustainable-development-goals--2 [Accessed 25 June 2024]
3. Welsh Government (2021) www.gov.wales/sites/default/files/publications/2021-02/future-wales-the-national-plan-2040.pdf [Accessed 25 June 2024]
4. United Nations Sustainable Development Goals, Communication Materials (2024) www.un.org/sustainabledevelopment/news/communications-material/ [Accessed 25 June 2024]
5. International Labour Organization (ILO) (2015) Decent work video. https://www.ilo.org/topics/decent-work [Accessed 16 July 2024]
6. Robertson, P. J. (2021) The contribution of career development to public policy objectives: Recognising the potential with the United Nations Sustainable Development Goals. CDI Briefing paper

7. Gatsby (2023) www.gatsby.org.uk/education/focus-areas/good-career-guidance [Accessed 25 June 2024]
8. Career Development Institute (2021) www.thecdi.net/resources/cdi-framework [Accessed 25 June 2024]
9. UK Parliament House of Commons Library (2023) https://commonslibrary.parliament.uk/halfway-to-2030-the-sustainable-development-goals/ [Accessed 25 June 2024]
10. UN Global Compact Network UK (2024) SDG showcase report. https://www.unglobalcompact.org.uk/wp-content/uploads/2024/03/SDG-Showcase-optimised-PDF.pdf

Chapter 3 - A sustainable career

1. Andrews, D. & Hooley, T. (2022) *The Careers Leader Handbook* (2nd Edition). Trotman, Bath.
2. Hall, D. T. & Mirvis, P. H. (1995) Careers as lifelong learning. In A. Howard (Ed.), *The changing nature of work* (pp. 323–361). Jossey-Bass/Wiley.
3. Arthur, M. B. & Rousseau, D. M. (1996) *The Boundaryless Career: A New Employment Principle for a New Organizational Era*. Oxford University Press.
4. De Vos, A., Van der Heijden, B. I. M. & Akkermans, J. (2020) Sustainable careers: towards a conceptual model. *Journal of Vocational Behaviour* 117, 103196. https://doi.org//10.1016/j.jvb.2018.06.011
5. Savickas, M. L. (1997) Career adaptability: An integrative construct for life-span, lifespace theory. *Career Development Quarterly* 45(3), 247
6. Bimrose, J., Brown, A., Barnes, S. & Hughes, D. (2011) The role of career adaptability in skills supply. Wath-upon-Dearne: UKCES (UK Commission for Employment and Skills). (UKCES Evidence Report).
7. Skills Development Scotland (2024) Career management skills. https://www.skillsdevelopmentscotland.co.uk/what-we-do/scotlands-careers-services/career-management-skills-explained [Accessed 22 July 2024]
8. IPSOS (July 2024) What worries the world? https://www.ipsos.com/sites/default/files/ct/news/documents/2024-07/What-Worries-the-World-July-2024.pdf [Accessed 30 July 2024]
9. International Labour Organization (2016) Decent work. https://www.ilo.org/topics/decent-work [Accessed 29 July 2024]
10. https://www.gov.scot/publications/young-peoples-experiences-precarious-flexible-work-main-report/pages/3/ [Accessed 29 July 2024]
11. Gallup (2024) Career wellbeing. https://www.gallup.com/topic/career-wellbeing.aspx [Accessed 29 July 2024]
12. Green Guidance (2024) Career support for sustainable life choices. https://www.green-guidance.eu/# [Accessed 29 July 2024]
13. UK Parliament (2024) Green skills for education and employment. https://post.parliament.uk/research-briefings/post-pn-0711/ [Accessed 29 July 2024]
14. Warwick Institute for Employment Research (2023) HE bridges 5.0. https://warwick.ac.uk/fac/soc/ier/researchthemesoverview/researchprojects/he_bridges/ [Accessed 14 January 2025]
15. Warwick Institute for Employment Research/University of Strathclyde (2022) Green jobs in Scotland: An inclusive approach to definition, measurement and analysis. https://www.skillsdevelopmentscotland.co.uk/media/q2lhglv5/green-jobs-in-scotland-report_final-4.pdf [Accessed 5 August 2024]
16. Nesta (2023) Expanding the green jobs sector – a quest to upskill the next generation. https://www.nesta.org.uk/blog/expanding-green-skills-training/ [Accessed 30 July 2024]

17. Deloitte (2024) 2024 Gen Z and millennial survey: Living and working with purpose in a transforming world. https://www.deloitte.com/global/en/issues/work/content/genz-millennialsurvey.html [Accessed 14 January 2025]

Chapter 4 - Careers in sustainability (Types of green jobs)

1. Warwick Institute for Employment Research/University of Strathclyde (2022) Green jobs in Scotland: An inclusive approach to definition, measurement and analysis. https://www.skillsdevelopmentscotland.co.uk/media/q2lhglv5/green-jobs-in-scotland-report_final-4.pdf [Accessed 5 August 2024]
2. UK Government (2021) Green jobs taskforce report. https://assets.publishing.service.gov.uk/media/650466aadec5be000dc35f85/green-jobs-taskforce-report-2021.pdf [Accessed 14 January 2025]
3. Office for National Statistics (14 March 2024) Statistical bulletin: Experimental estimates of green jobs. https://www.ons.gov.uk/economy/environmentalaccounts/bulletins/experimentalestimatesofgreenjobsuk/2024 [Accessed 3 September 2024]
4. US Bureau of Labor Statistics (2010) Measuring green jobs. https://www.bls.gov/green/home.htm#definition [Accessed 5 August 2024]
5. Office for National Statistics (2023) The current standard occupational classification for the UK (SOC 2020) https://www.ons.gov.uk/methodology/classificationsandstandards/standardoccupationalclassificationsoc/soc2020 [Accessed 29 August 2024]

Chapter 5 - Sectors Getting Us to Net Zero

1. United Nations (2024) Climate change: Net zero. www.un.org/en/climatechange/net-zero-coalition [Accessed 3 December 2024]
2. UK Parliament (2024) Research briefing: The UK's plans and progress to reach net zero by 2050. https://commonslibrary.parliament.uk/research-briefings/cbp-9888/ [Accessed 3 December 2024]
3. Energy UK (2024) The voice of the energy industry. https://www.energy-uk.org.uk/ [Accessed 3 December 2024]
4. National Grid (2020) Building the net zero energy workforce report. www.nationalgrid.com/stories/journey-to-net-zero/net-zero-energy-workforce [Accessed 3 December 2024]
5. UK Government (2024) Department for energy security and net zero. www.gov.uk/government/organisations/department-for-energy-security-and-net-zero/about [Accessed 3 December 2024]
6. UK Government (2024) Great British energy. https://great-british-energy.org.uk/ [Accessed 3 December 2024]
7. BBC Bitesize (2024) Crude oil and hydrocarbons. www.bbc.co.uk/bitesize/guides/zshvw6f/revision/1 [Accessed 3 December 2024]
8. UK Government (2024) News story: Updated oil and gas guidance following Supreme Court ruling. www.gov.uk/government/news/updated-oil-and-gas-guidance-following-supreme-court-ruling [Accessed 3 December 2024]
9. Uswitch (2024) UK renewable energy statistics 2024. www.uswitch.com/gas-electricity/studies/renewable-statistics [Accessed 3 December 2024]
10. Low Carbon Contract Company (2024) What is green hydrogen? www.lowcarboncontracts.uk/our-schemes/low-carbon-hydrogen/ [Accessed 5 December 2024]

11. Durham Energy Institute (2024) Hydrogen and fuel cell research. https://durham.ac.uk/research/institutes-and-centres/durham-energy-institute/research--impact/research-themes/energy-infrastructure-and-systems/hydrogen/ [Accessed 5 December 2024]
12. HM Government (2023) Powering up Britain. https://assets.publishing.service.gov.uk/media/642468ff2fa8480013ec0f39/powering-up-britain-joint-overview.pdf [Accessed 5 December 2024]
13. Energy UK (2024) How the retail market works. www.energy-uk.org.uk/insights/how-the-retail-market-works/ [Accessed 5 December 2024]
14. BBC News (12 September 2024) Data centres as vital as NHS and power grid, government says. www.bbc.co.uk/news/articles/c23ljy4z05mo [Accessed 5 December 2024]
15. UK Government (3 November 2023) News story: Thousands of homes to be kept warm by waste heat from computer data centres in UK first. www.gov.uk/government/news/thousands-of-homes-to-be-kept-warm-by-waste-heat-from-computer-data-centres-in-uk-first [Accessed 5 December 2024]
16. Water UK (2024) Climate change: The water industry is playing its part in tackling climate change. www.water.org.uk/protecting-environment/climate-change [Accessed 5 December 2024]
17. Murray McIntosh (April 2024) The water industry labour report 2024. www.murraymcintosh.com/water/article/key-insights-from-the-water-industry-employment-report [Accessed 5 December 2024]
18. Stastica (2024) Employment in the waste collection, treatment, and disposal sector in the United Kingdom (UK) from 2010 to 2022. https://www.statista.com/statistics/1446949/waste-management-employment-uk/ [Accessed 17 December 2024]
19. Waste Managed (2024) What actually happens to rubbish in the UK? www.wastemanaged.co.uk/our-news/other/what-actually-happens-to-rubbish-in-the-uk/ [Accessed 5 December 2024]
20. Department for Environment, Food and Rural Affairs (26 September 24) UK statistics on waste. www.gov.uk/government/statistics/uk-waste-data/uk-statistics-on-waste [Accessed 5 December 2024]
21. Ellen MacArthur Foundation (2024) Circular economy introduction. https://www.ellenmacarthurfoundation.org/topics/circular-economy-introduction/overview [Accessed 17 December 2024]
22. Chartered Institution of Wastes Management (2024) (2024) Turning off the tap: Why better design can increase resource resilience and reduce consumption. https://www.circularonline.co.uk/wp-content/uploads/2024/06/Root_CIWM_PresidentialReport_Final-Issued_v4.pdf [Accessed 17 December 2024]
23. Natural England (2024) State of natural capital report for England 2024. https://nbn.org.uk/wp-content/uploads/2024/11/NERR137-Edition-1-State-of-Natural-Capital-Report-for-England-2024-Risks-to-nature-and-why-it-matters.pdf [Accessed 17 December 2024]
24. UK Government (22 February 2024) Understanding biodiversity net gain. www.gov.uk/guidance/understanding-biodiversity-net-gain [Accessed 19 December 2024]
25. IUCN (2024) UK peatland programme. www.iucn-uk-peatlandprogramme.org/peatland-code-0 [Accessed 19 December 2024]
26. Climate Change Committee (July 2024) Progress towards reaching Net Zero in the UK. www.theccc.org.uk/climate-action/uk-action-on-climate-change/progress-snapshot/ [Accessed 19 December 2024]
27. The Flood Hub (2024) Natural flood management (NFM). https://thefloodhub.co.uk/nfm/ [Accessed 19 December 2024]

28. UK Government (5 November 2024) Natural flood management programme. www.gov.uk/guidance/natural-flood-management-programme [Accessed 19 December 2024]
29. Lantra (2024) Introduction to environmental conservation. www.lantra.co.uk/careers/Industry/Environmental%20Conservation [Accessed 17 December 2024]

Chapter 6 - Sectors working in a sustainable way

1. Mineral Matters (2023) Labour market intelligence survey. https://minerals-matter.co.uk/wp-content/uploads/Labour-Market-Intelligence-Survey-2023-web-version.pdf [Accessed 13 August 2024]
2. Sustain (2024) Careers in sustainable food and farming. https://www.sustainweb.org/reports/may24-careers-in-sustainable-food-and-farming/ [Accessed 13 August 2024]
3. National Food Strategy (2019) The plan. https://www.nationalfoodstrategy.org/ [Accessed 13 August 2024]
4. UK Government (2024) Green financing allocation report. https://www.gov.uk/government/publications/uk-government-green-financing-allocation-report-2024 [Accessed 26 November 2024]
5. UK Green Building Council (2024) https://ukgbc.org/
6. Make UK (2024) UK manufacturing: The facts 2024. https://www.makeuk.org/insights/publications [Accessed 15 August 2024]
7. Make UK (2024) Future factories powered by AI. https://www.makeuk.org/insights/reports/future-factories-powered-ai [Accessed 26 November 2024]
8. Barclays Corporate (2024) Insights: Exploring the skills shortage in UK Manufacturing. www.barclayscorporate.com/insights/industry-expertise/skills-shortage-in-uk-manufacturing/ [Accessed 26 November 2024]
9. Make UK (2024) ESG in manufacturing. https://www.makeuk.org/insights/reports/2024/01/29/esg-in-manufacturing [Accessed 26 November 2024]
10. Lancet Countdown (2023) 2023 global report. https://www.lancetcountdown.org/2023-report/ [Accessed 20 August 2024]
11. World Health Organization (2017) Environmentally sustainable health systems: A strategic document https://www.who.int/publications/i/item/WHO-EURO-2017-2241-41996-57723 [Accessed 20 August 2024]
12. NHS England (2022) Delivering a 'Net Zero' national health service. https://www.england.nhs.uk/greenernhs/a-net-zero-nhs/ [Accessed 20 August 2024]
13. PresQIPP (October 2021) Inhaler carbon footprint. https://www.prescqipp.info/our-resources/bulletins/bulletin-295-inhaler-carbon-footprint/ [Accessed 26 November 2024]
14. UK government (2024) Sectors – The UK's cutting-edge technology and revolutionary research is leading the race to a net zero carbon economy. https://www.great.gov.uk/international/investment/sectors/ [Accessed 26 November 2024]
15. Lab, U. & Mattila, V. & Pang, R. (2023) How gaming can be more sustainable?. https://doi.org/10.37602/UN1TY.2023.53100.

Further reading

- For regular updates about sectors, employment and the UK economy https://www.lloydsbank.com/business/resource-centre/insight/uk-sector-tracker.html
- NICE (National Institute for Health and Care Excellence) has global and UK information about why the health care sector must work more sustainably and how this can be achieved. https://www.nice.org.uk/about/who-we-are/sustainability

Chapter 7 – Qualifications in Sustainability

1. University College London (2024) Teaching for sustainable futures, centre for climate change and sustainability education. https://www.ucl.ac.uk/ioe/departments-and-centres/centres/centre-climate-change-and-sustainability-education/teaching-sustainable-futures [Accessed 17 September 2024]
2. Future Learn (2024) Introduction to teaching sustainability and climate action. https://www.futurelearn.com/courses/teaching-sustainability-climate-action-in-schools [Accessed 17 September 2024]
3. UNESCO (2020) Sustainability starts with teachers. https://course.sustainabilityteachers.org/ [Accessed 17 September 2024]
4. Education and Training Foundation (2024) Education for sustainable development. https://www.et-foundation.co.uk/resources/esd/ [Accessed 17 September 2024]
5. Energising Futures (2024) Green skills unlocked. https://energisingfutures.co.uk/green-skills-unlocked/ [Accessed 17 September 2024]
6. Jones, M. (2021) British education research association. Developing a sustainable Wales and beyond. [Accessed 24 September 2024] https://www.bera.ac.uk/blog/developing-a-sustainable-wales-and-beyond
7. Welsh Government (2022) Welsh baccalaureate guidance. https://www.gov.wales/welsh-baccalaureate [Accessed 17 September 2024]
8. Sustrans (2024) The global citizenship challenge Welsh baccalaureate KS4: A guide for teachers. https://www.sustrans.org.uk/media/3071/welsh-bacc_teachernotes_engfinal.pdf [Accessed 17 September 2024]
9. Pearson (2021) Meeting the challenge of climate change through project learning. www.pearson.com/content/dam/one-dot-com/one-dot-com/uk/documents/subjects/humanities/blog-climate-change.pdf [Accessed 17 September 2024]
10. OCR (2024) GCSE in natural history. https://teach.ocr.org.uk/naturalhistory [Accessed 17 September 2024]

Chapter 8 – Rising to the challenge

1. Marciniak, J., Johnston, C. S., Steiner, R. S. & Hirschi, A. (2022) Career preparedness among adolescents: A review of key components and directions for future research. *Journal of Career Development*, 49(1), 18–40. https://doi.org/10.1177/0894845320943951 [Accessed 7 October 2024]
2. Climate Change Committee (2024) Progress towards reaching net zero. https://www.theccc.org.uk/uk-action-on-climate-change/progress-snapshot/ [Accessed 7 October 2024]
3. Mental Health UK (2023) https://mentalhealth-uk.org/blog/what-is-climate-anxiety-and-what-can-we-do-about-it [Accessed 7 October 2024]
4. Carbon Credits.com (2024) The ultimate guide to understanding carbon credits. https://carboncredits.com/the-ultimate-guide-to-understanding-carbon-credits [Accessed 8 October 2024]
5. UK Government (2024) Participating in the UK emissions trading scheme. https://www.gov.uk/government/publications/participating-in-the-uk-ets [Accessed 8 October 2024]
6. Greenpeace (2022) Greenwash: What it is and how not to fall for it. https://www.greenpeace.org.uk/news/what-is-greenwashing/ [Accessed 8 October 2024]
7. UK Extractive Industries Transparency Initiative (2024) Oil and gas in the UK. https://www.ukeiti.org/ [Accessed 8 October 2024]

8. International Association of Oil & Gas Producers (2024) Oil in everyday life. https://www.iogp.org/workstreams/advocacy/oil-in-everyday-life/ [Accessed 8 October 2024]
9. Machinery Lubrication (2023) Sustainability and eco-friendly lubricants: A new frontier in lubrication programs. https://www.machinerylubrication.com/Read/32527/sustainability-eco-friendly-lubricants-new-frontier-in-lube-programs [Accessed 8 October 2024]
10. Donald, W. E., Baruch, Y. & Ashleigh, M. J. (2024) Construction and operationalisation of an employability capital growth model (ECGM) via a systematic literature review (2016–2022). *Studies in Higher Education* 49(1), 1–15. https://doi.org/10.1080/03075079.2023.2219270
11. Nesta (2018) Making sense of skills: a UK skills taxonomy. https://data-viz.nesta.org.uk/skills-taxonomy/index.html [Accessed 8 October 2024]
12. UK Government (2024) Occupations in demand. https://explore-education-statistics.service.gov.uk/find-statistics/occupations-in-demand/2024 [Accessed 8 October 2024]
13. Career Development Institute (2024) CDI code of ethics. https://www.thecdi.net/about-us/cdi-code-of-ethics [Accessed 10 October 2024]
14. UK Government (2021) Social mobility barometer. https://www.gov.uk/government/publications/social-mobility-barometer-2021 [Accessed 10 October 2024]
15. National Youth Entrepreneurship Challenge (2024) The entrepreneurial mindset. https://nfte.com/entrepreneurial-mindset/ [Accessed 10 October 2024]

Further reading

- UK Government (2021) The eccy: Carbon offsetting- reviewing the evidence. https://environmentagency.blog.gov.uk/2021/05/10/carbon-offsetting-reviewing-the-evidence/ [Accessed 8 October 2024]
- CIPD (2023) Sickness absence rate jumps to the highest in a decade. https://www.cipd.org/uk/views-and-insights/thought-leadership/cipd-voice/sickness-absence-rate-jumps/
- Bellehumeur, C. R., Carignan, L. & Robinson, N. (2024) Acceptance and commitment therapy to alleviate climate-induced psychological distress. https://www.tandfonline.com/doi/epdf/10.1080/03069885.2024.2384745?needAccess=true
- Employability Capital Growth Model (ECGM; Donald et al., 2024) https://myfuture.edu.au/docs/default-source/insights/the_employability_capital_growth_model.pdf?sfvrsn=31b136db_1
- Das, L (2022) Greenpeace. Climate anxiety: 21 resources to energise you into action. https://www.greenpeace.org.uk/news/climate-anxiety-resources-to-energise-action/

Chapter 9 – Sustainability and Career Education

1. UNESCO (2020) Education for sustainable development: A roadmap. https://unesdoc.unesco.org/ark:/48223/pf0000374802 [Accessed 14 October 2024]
2. United Nations (2024) Sustainable development: The 17 goals. https://sdgs.un.org/goals [Accessed 14 October 2024]
3. Hill, I (2023) The open university blog. What is most important when integrating 'green skills' and sustainability topics into learning and teaching strategies? https://www5.open.ac.uk/scholarship-and-innovation/scilab/blog/how-to-intergrate-green-skills-and-sustainability-topics-into-teaching-and-learning-strategies [Accessed 4 November 2024]

4. CDI (2024) Career development framework. www.thecdi.net/resources/cdi-framework [Accessed 14 October 2024]
5. Dimsits, M. & Hooley, T. (2024) Introduction to the framework for environmentally sustainable career guidance. Presentation delivered at the *NICEC conference on sustainability and career*, Birmingham, 2–3rd July 2024. https://www.nicec.org/pages/2024-conference-videos [Accessed 3 March 2025]
6. British Educational Research Association (2021) Research commission 2019/2020: Manifesto for education for environmental sustainability (EfES). www.bera.ac.uk/publication/bera-research-commission-2019-2020-manifesto-for-education-for-environmental-sustainability-efes [Accessed 4 November 2024]
7. NCVO (2024) Theory of change. https://www.ncvo.org.uk/help-and-guidance/strategy-and-impact/strategy-and-business-planning/theory-of-change [Accessed 4 November 2024]
8. Neyt, B., Omey, E., Verhaest, D. & Baert, S. (2019) Does student work really affect educational outcomes? A review of the literature. *Journal of Economic Surveys* 33(3), 896–921. https://doi.org/10.1111/joes.12301
9. Ho, C. T. Y. (2024) Enhancing a career development curriculum by embedding the United Nations sustainable development goals. *Journal of the National Institute for Career Education and Counselling* 53(1), 24–35. https://doi.org/10.20856/jnicec.5304

Further reading

- Department for Education (2023) Policy paper. Sustainability and climate change: A strategy for the education and children's services systems. www.gov.uk/government/publications/sustainability-and-climate-change-strategy/9317e6ed-6c80-4eb9-be6d-3fcb1f232f3a
- Nuttall, B. (2024) Green career education and guidance through the perceptions and experiences of career practitioners in English secondary schools. *Journal of the National Institute for Career Education and Counselling* 53(1), 105–121. https://doi.org/10.20856/jnicec.5310
- For more information about a number of sustainability in education initiatives read the 2021 blog from The British Educational Research Association (BERA) www.bera.ac.uk/blog-special-issues/embedding-sustainability-education-in-practice

For more information about Action Learning Sets and transformational change visit

- www.et-foundation.co.uk/wp-content/uploads/2022/06/ETF-guide-to-action-learning-sets.pdf
- www.leedsbeckett.ac.uk/blogs/carnegie-education/2022/03/action-learning-sets-a-pedagogic-and-professional-tool/
- www.aihr.com/hr-glossary/transformational-change/

Chapter 10 – Wrapping up

1. WRAP (2024) https://www.wrap.ngo/ [Accessed 21 November 2024]
2. Stockholm Resilience Centre (2024) Planetary boundaries. https://www.stockholmresilience.org/research/planetary-boundaries.html [Accessed 21 November 2024]
3. Donald, W. E., Van der Heijden, B. I. J. M. & Baruch, Y. (2024) Introducing a sustainable career ecosystem: Theoretical perspectives, conceptualization, and

future research agenda. *Journal of Vocational Behavior* 151, 103989. https://doi.org/10.1016/j.jvb.2024.103989

4. Sabates, R., Harris, A. L. & Staff, J. (2011) Ambition gone awry: The long-term socioeconomic consequences of misaligned and uncertain ambitions in adolescence. *Social Science Quarterly (Wiley-Blackwell)* 92(4), 959–977. https://doi.org/10.1111/j.1540-6237.2011.00799.x

5. Mousteri, V., Daly, M. & Delaney, L. (2018) The scarring effect of unemployment on psychological wellbeing across Europe. *Social Science Research* 72, 146–169. DOI:10.1016/j.ssresearch.2018.01.007

www.ingramcontent.com/pod-product-compliance
Lightning Source LLC
Chambersburg PA
CBHW061118010526
44112CB00024B/2909